# MODERN *hospitality*

## SIMPLE RECIPES
## with SOUTHERN CHARM

from the winner of Season 1
**MasterChef**

# WHITNEY MILLER

RODALE

THE ADVOCATE COLLECTION

Rodale books may be purchased for business or
promotional use or for special sales. For information,
please write to: Special Markets Department, Rodale
Inc., 733 Third Avenue, New York, NY 10017.

Printed in the United States of America
Rodale Inc. makes every effort to use acid-free ♾, 
recycled paper ♲.

Book design by Kara Plikaitis
Photographs by Ellen Silverman
Recipe cards courtesy of Rifle Paper Company

**Library of Congress Cataloging-in-Publication Data
is on file with the publisher.**
ISBN-10: 1-60961-352-X
ISBN-13: 978-1-60961-352-5

**Distributed to the trade by Macmillan**
2  4  6  8  10  9  7  5  3  1  hardcover

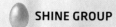     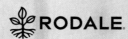

FOX™ FOX and its related entities.
All rights reserved.

The MasterChef logo and the
MasterChef "M-Swirl" logo are
trademarks of Shine Limited and used
under license. All rights reserved.

We inspire and enable people to improve their lives and the world around them.
www.rodalebooks.com

# MODERN
# hospitality

### To my mom, Mary

I could not have completed this cookbook without you. Thank you for the many nights you stayed up helping me test, taste, and wash dishes. And thank you for sharing your gift of creative writing with me.

I love you!

### To my great-grandmother, Mary Strahan

Since I was a young girl, I've admired the way you demonstrate hospitality to others. Whether it's a glass of sweet tea or a slice of cake, you always have something to offer a guest.

Thank you for sharing your secrets to Southern cooking with me.

### To my Lord and Savior

I am so thankful for the gift of cooking you have given me. Thank you for blessing me with the opportunity to write this cookbook, which has always been my dream.

"Each one should use whatever gift he has received to serve others . . ."
1 PETER 4:10

···········

## Foreword by
# GORDON RAMSAY

I MET WHITNEY MILLER ON DAY 2 of the first season of the FOX show, *MasterChef*. My fellow judges Graham Elliot and Joe Bastianich and I had already tasted umpteen dozens upon dozens of amazing home-cooked dishes from very talented and determined amateur cooks with no professional culinary training. By the time Whitney presented her dish to us, she had some pretty tough acts to follow. At just 22 years of age, Whitney practically tiptoed into the *MasterChef* kitchen. We all thought she was a sweet lamb heading toward inevitable slaughter.

That first dish Whitney made for us, Blackened Catfish Tacos with Mango Chutney, was absolutely delicious. I was impressed, but I expected that her age and lack of life experience would trip her up along the way. In short, I wasn't convinced that she was ready to handle the pressure of the *MasterChef* challenges that were to follow. I asked her if anyone had come to Los Angeles with her for support and soon found myself bombarded with a barrage of pure Mississippian passion in the

# *modern flair...*

form of Mom, Dad, and little sister Brittyn. They begged me to understand that while Whitney might look sweet and innocent, she was also a brilliant cook and a true fighter; ready, willing, and able for any culinary battle that lay ahead. On the back of such forceful family support, Graham, Joe, and I decided she might have more to show us. How right we were.

Whitney went on to eliminate each and every contender and win the title of America's first MasterChef. Her signature Southern-style appetizers and entrées showcased a fresh, modern flair, and her desserts were technically brilliant as well as delicious. She truly nailed her competition at every turn. From her melt-in-your-mouth venison with gravy to perfect profiteroles, Whitney's youthful spirit and take-no-prisoners approach certainly made me sit up and take notice.

In the months since Whitney took the *MasterChef* crown, she's gone on to open a successful café and catering company in her hometown of Poplarville. She's given cooking demos alongside Cat Cora and Emeril Lagasse. And now she's published her first cookbook. Not bad for 23!

I love the food of the southern United States. In my own personal trips through Mississippi and Louisiana, I've enjoyed some of the best dishes and locally grown produce that this incredibly diverse region has to offer. The South has a reputation for deep-fried chicken, grits, and heavy comfort food, but I've always thought there was room for a more modern, less heavy-handed approach to these familiar classics. I am proud to say that Whitney, a University of Southern Mississippi graduate with a concentration in nutrition and biology, is an exciting new culinary voice who is reinterpreting many wonderful Southern dishes into fresh, simple, and absolutely delicious recipes for today's generation of home cooks.

I hope that you and your family enjoy creating recipes and taking inspiration from Whitney's brilliant first book. I personally love the Oven-Fried Catfish with Fresh Dill Tartar Sauce recipe on page 89. I think you will, too!

– GORDON RAMSAY

*...technically brilliant*

Old fashioned oatmeal
cookies.

Spice cake mix.
1 pk spice cake mix
2 cups uncooked oatmeal
2 eggs.
½ cup cooking oil
⅔ cup milk
2 cups ~~raisins~~ raisins
1 cup chopped nuts
¼ cup dark brown sugar.
                    Tem - 350°
until brown.

Carrot Souffle'
2 c. softened mashed carrots or baby food to
        equal 2 cups
1 stick butter
2 eggs beaten
3 tablespoons flour
1 tsp Baking Powder
1 cup sugar
pinch of cinnamon
Blend together bake at 400° for
15 then 350° for 45 min

BUTTER
1 pkg P. SUGAR
2 Cups

1 6³ Oz Frozen
        Orange Juice
mix + add

1 Box of crushed
V. wafers.
Roll in Ball's +
roll in Coconut.
Keep in Ice Box

Pepper
12 sweet peppers
12 "
3 large Onions
3 tablespoons salt
2 pints vinegar
2 cups sugar and
Chop peppers fine
Cover with boiling
water. Let stand
10 min. Drain. Co
again with boiling
water and let come
to a boil. Let stand
again for 10 min. Drain
well & add sugar, salt
& vinegar. Heat to boiling
reduce heat and simmer
for 15 min. Pack in hot
jars. Seal

# Introduction

THOUGH I CONSIDER MYSELF to be a relatively modern woman, I'm the product of a very traditional Southern background. Growing up in the small (as in one-traffic-light small) town of Poplarville, Mississippi, I spent most of my free time in the kitchen with my mother and grandmothers. In the summertime I foraged in the woods for fresh blackberries that we'd use to make cobblers, muffins, and pancakes; I gathered pecans with my friend Rebecca for pies, brownies, and just about everything else; and I picked zucchini in my friend Lara's garden that would be used to make bread.

I also spent plenty of carefree afternoons walking barefoot in the grass and jumping over a sprinkler (a backyard Southern waterfall) or sitting on the porch with my friends eating thick wedges of fresh watermelon, bowls of homemade ice cream, and shelled peas straight from the garden.

# These recipes embody the tradition and spirit of home-style

Today I still live with my family on our 7 acres of land in Poplarville, and I still pick wild berries in the summer and tend our garden of fruits, vegetables, and herbs with my dad. But these days, after becoming the first US winner of *MasterChef*, I am just as likely to be found sampling the menu at a trendy restaurant as donning an apron and, covered in flour, whipping up a feast for family and friends. I am passionate about food and cooking; I love traveling throughout the country and tasting what our best restaurants have to offer, what today's chefs are dreaming up and serving. But even more than that, I love cooking and serving my food to others. It was so exciting to see my recipes, along with those of my fellow contestants, published in the *MasterChef Cookbook* in 2010. And now I am thrilled to have a cookbook of my own.

The art of hospitality and entertaining is a long-standing Southern tradition—one that's been passed down through generations of women in my family (along with the recipes for the best biscuits and cornbread you'll ever taste). Ever since I was a little girl, hospitality, faith, fellowship, and food have been at the heart of our family activities. After church on Sundays, we often visited my 95-year-old great-grandma's house for lunch along with other family members and friends. Heaping plates of perfect flaky biscuits were passed around the table and topped with cane syrup and butter; a huge

# Southern cooking and hospitality.

pot roast (hospitality meant always having plenty of food to share) was carved and later turned into a week's worth of leftovers; for dessert, ample servings of sky-high fluffy lemon meringue pie were scooped onto plates and quickly disappeared And, of course, the whole meal was washed down with gallons of sweet tea.

In this—my very first cookbook—you'll find updated versions of recipes that have been lovingly prepared and served by four generations of women in my family, as well as my own signature creations. You'll notice that many of these traditional dishes have a decidedly modern twist, but at their essence, these recipes embody the tradition and spirit of home-style Southern cooking and hospitality.

You'll also find plenty of tips for entertaining throughout these pages—whether it's serving Loaded Fingerling Potato Skins (page 29) and Game-Day Chili (page 46) for a crowd of rowdy football fans or hosting a ladies' luncheon with Lemon-Pepper Chicken Salad (page 50) and Toasted Coconut Cupcakes with Lemon Glaze (page 127), I share my favorite tips for creating instant ambiance. It's easy to transform an everyday occasion into something special without a lot of extra fuss. The art

of hospitality is all about making your guests feel welcome, comfortable, and at home. I feel so blessed to have been a part of *MasterChef*–an experience that not only allowed my culinary skills to grow and shine but also my faith in Christ. And while I'm incredibly grateful for the exciting opportunities that have come my way since winning the grand prize, no matter where I travel, dine, or cook, hosting and feeding the people I love remains one of my greatest joys in life. As you look through the pages of my cookbook, I hope you are inspired to invite your own loved ones over to share a meal and create new memories and traditions.

My family and I wish you and your family lots of fun in the kitchen!

*Whitney Miller*

*1*

# RISE AND
# SHINE

When spending the night at my great-grandmother's house to go hunting, my dad would try to sneak out to the deer stand at daybreak. Just as his hand touched the doorknob, Grandma Strahan would say, "John, have you eaten breakfast?" Of course he hadn't, so nothing would do but for him to sit down to a full Southern breakfast of eggs, grits, bacon, and fluffy biscuits. By then the sun was out.

# Fresh Fruit and Granola Tarts

You often see fruit, yogurt, and granola parfaits on breakfast menus. In my version of this breakfast staple, I've created granola tart shells that can easily be prepared ahead of time for entertaining at brunch or lunch. The presentation makes this easy-to-assemble dish feel like something special.

2 cups old-fashioned rolled oats

6 tablespoons light brown sugar

6 tablespoons chopped pecans

$1/2$ teaspoon ground cinnamon

$1/4$ teaspoon salt

6 tablespoons cane syrup or maple syrup

4 tablespoons ($1/2$ stick) unsalted butter, melted

2 cups strawberries, sliced

$1 1/3$ cup blueberries

2 large bananas, sliced

$1 1/2$ cups whole-milk plain yogurt

2 teaspoons honey (optional)

1 tablespoon grated orange zest

Preheat the oven to 325°F.

Combine the oats, brown sugar, pecans, cinnamon, salt, syrup, and butter in a medium bowl. Divide the mixture evenly among three $4 1/2$-inch tart pans with removable bottoms. Press the mixture into the bottom, but not the sides, of the tart pans. Bake for 10 minutes. Remove from the oven and using the back of a spoon, press some of the granola into the sides of the tart pans. Return to the oven to bake for 3 to 5 minutes to set the crust.

Let the tart shells rest for 3 to 4 minutes, then, using an oven mitt to protect the hand holding the tart pan, carefully remove the tart shells from the pans and place on a rack to cool.

Toss together the strawberries, blueberries, and bananas in a medium bowl.

To serve, place each tart shell on a small plate. Spoon the fruit mixture into the shells. Top each with a $1/4$ cup yogurt. Drizzle with honey, if desired. Serve garnished with orange zest.

Makes 6 tarts

# Biscuits and Cane Syrup

My great-grandmother used to make biscuits in a carved wooden bowl known as a "dough bowl," which is used for making bread in the South. The art of biscuit making was passed down through generations in my family. These biscuits have the perfect texture—flaky and delicate, with a crunchy bottom. They're delicious for breakfast with sweet syrup and can be paired with gravy for a satisfying, savory dish. My mom likes to enjoy her biscuits with softened butter and cane syrup mixed together!

1 cup self-rising flour

2 tablespoons butter-flavored shortening, chilled

⅓ cup whole milk

1 tablespoon canola oil

2 tablespoons unsalted butter, melted

Softened butter and cane syrup, for serving

Preheat the oven to 425°F.

Place the flour in a medium bowl. Using a pastry cutter or a fork, cut the shortening into the flour. Stir in the milk until incorporated. Lightly flour your hands and form the dough into a ball. Divide the dough into 4 portions. Form each portion into a smooth ball by rolling it between your palms 5 times. Tuck any rough edges into the top of the ball. Roll between your hands 10 more times to form a smooth ball. Repeat with the other 3 portions.

Grease a cast-iron griddle with the oil. Place a dough ball, smoother side down, in the pan to coat with oil and flip over so that the smooth side is facing up. With three fingers, press the dough down a bit, making a slight indention on the top of each biscuit.

Bake until golden brown, 16 to 18 minutes. Remove from the oven and brush the tops of the warm biscuits with the melted butter.

Serve the biscuits warm with softened butter and cane syrup.

Makes 4 biscuits

# Breakfast Grit Cakes

In the South, grits are traditionally prepared on the stovetop with butter, salt, and pepper. In this recipe, cooked grits are transformed into cakes that serve as a base for eggs, bacon, and cheese. But you can top these simple little cakes with anything you'd like. If you're serving breakfast for a crowd, simply set out a platter of grits cakes alongside bowls of toppings and let your guests assemble their own creations.

$2\frac{1}{3}$ cups water

1 cup quick-cooking grits

5 tablespoons unsalted butter

1 teaspoon salt

$\frac{1}{8}$ teaspoon ground black pepper

$\frac{1}{8}$ teaspoon cayenne pepper (optional)

$\frac{1}{3}$ cup all-purpose flour

Dad's Scrambled Eggs (page 13)

5 slices bacon, cooked and crumbled

$\frac{1}{4}$ cup sliced grape tomatoes

$\frac{3}{4}$ cup shredded sharp Cheddar cheese

2 tablespoons sliced scallions

Bring $2\frac{1}{3}$ cups water to a boil in a medium saucepan over high heat. Stir in the grits, reduce the heat to low, and cook, stirring occasionally, until grits reach porridge consistency, about 5 minutes. Remove from the heat and stir in 2 tablespoons of the butter, the salt, black pepper, and cayenne (if using).

Line a pizza pan or small rimmed baking sheet with plastic wrap. Pour the grits in the center of the pan. Using a spatula, spread the grits evenly to a thickness of $\frac{3}{8}$ inch. Let cool until the grits are set, about 30 minutes.

Using a 3-inch round cookie or biscuit cutter, cut out 12 circles from the cooled grits. Dredge both sides of the grits cakes in flour.

Heat a large cast-iron pan over medium-high heat. Melt 2 tablespoons of the butter in the pan swirl to coat the bottom. Working with half the cakes at a time, cook until lightly browned, $1\frac{1}{2}$ to 2 minutes per side. Carefully remove with a spatula and drain on a paper towel–lined baking sheet. Add the remaining 1 tablespoon butter to the pan and cook the remaining cakes.

Preheat the broiler. Line a broiler pan with foil.

Place the cakes on the broiler pan. Spoon the scrambled eggs onto the cakes. Top with the bacon, tomatoes, and cheese. Broil until the cheese melts, 1 to 2 minutes.

Place the grits cakes on a serving platter. Sprinkle with the scallions. Serve hot.

Serves 6

# Upside-Down Quiches

Omelets are a favorite breakfast food in my family, but who has time to stand over the stove and prepare omelets "made to order" all morning? Not me! In this easy recipe, you simply pour all of your favorite omelet ingredients into ramekins and make mini-quiches. To add contrast to the soft egg texture, I top my baked "omelets" with a crispy biscuit crust.

## BISCUIT CRUST

1 cup self-rising flour

2 tablespoons butter-flavored shortening, chilled

1/4 teaspoon chopped fresh rosemary

1/2 cup low-fat buttermilk

1 tablespoons unsalted butter, melted (for the ramekins)

## FILLING

8 large eggs

1 1/3 cups half-and-half

3/4 teaspoon salt

1/4 teaspoon ground black pepper

4 teaspoons diced yellow onion

4 tablespoons diced green or red bell peppers

4 heaping tablespoons diced chopped cremini mushrooms

4 tablespoons cooked and crumbled fresh andouille sausage or bacon

8 tablespoons shredded sharp Cheddar cheese or feta cheese

Preheat the oven to 375°F. Lightly coat four 8-ounce ramekins with cooking spray and place on a baking sheet.

To make the biscuit crust: Place the flour in a medium bowl. Using a pastry cutter or fork, cut the shortening into the flour. Stir in the rosemary and buttermilk until incorporated. Flour your hands and lightly form the dough into a ball. Cover with plastic wrap and refrigerate for 10 minutes.

Sprinkle flour over a clean surface. Roll the dough out to a 1/4-inch-thick round. Using a 5-inch round object, trace and cut out 4 rounds.

To make the filling: Beat the eggs in a large bowl. Whisk in the half-and-half, salt, and black pepper.

Dividing evenly, layer the remaining ingredients into the ramekins in this order: onion, bell pepper, mushrooms, sausage (or bacon), cheese. Evenly distribute the egg mixture among the ramekins.

Coat the rims of the ramekins with a little bit of the melted butter to help the biscuit crust stick. Place the biscuit dough rounds onto the tops of the ramekins and gently press the dough onto the rims and against the sides. Brush the tops of the crusts with the remaining melted butter.

Bake until the crust is golden brown, 20 to 25 minutes. Let quiches sit for 5 minutes before serving.

Serves 4

# Cinnamon and Pecan Granola

Rolled oats are one of my favorite breakfast food ingredients—I love a hot bowl of oatmeal in the morning, and I often use oats in my baking, as well. But most of all I like using oats in this quick and easy granola recipe. You can make a batch on a Monday and enjoy it throughout the week. I like to sprinkle it over my yogurt for a sweet start to the morning.

1 cup old-fashioned rolled oats

3 tablespoons light brown sugar

3 tablespoons chopped pecans

2 tablespoons dried cranberries or blueberries

¼ teaspoon ground cinnamon

⅛ teaspoon salt

3 tablespoons cane syrup or maple syrup

2 tablespoons unsalted butter, melted

Preheat the oven to 325°F.

Toss together the oats, brown sugar, pecans, berries, cinnamon, salt, syrup, and butter in a medium bowl.

Pour the granola onto a baking sheet and bake for 10 minutes. Remove from the oven, loosen and mix the granola with a spoon, and return to the oven and bake until golden brown, 12 to 15 minutes. Remove from the oven and toss the granola again. Let cool before serving or storing.

Serve granola in a bowl with fresh fruit and milk or yogurt.

Makes about 1½ cups

Don't wait for holidays or important occasions to add special touches to meals. I like to use inexpensive stemmed goblets and pretty or unusual dishes, even for a weekday breakfast. They add a beautiful touch to family meals.

# Dad's Scrambled Eggs

At my house, it's not unusual to have breakfast for dinner. Everyone gets in the kitchen and cooks his or her specialty and then we have an evening breakfast feast! My mom and I team up and make biscuits and andouille gravy (see the gravy that goes with the Creamy Mashed Potatoes on page 75). My dad always makes his famous scrambled eggs. His technique produces such fluffy eggs that I like to call these "pillows-in-your-mouth."

5 large eggs

¼ teaspoon salt

⅛ teaspoon ground black pepper

Whisk the eggs and 2 tablespoons water in a medium bowl until combined. Whisk in the salt and pepper.

Coat the bottom of a 12-inch nonstick skillet with cooking spray and heat over medium-high heat. Pour in the egg mixture. Cook, without stirring, until bubbles begin to form, 30 seconds to 1 minute. When bubbles begin to form, gently scrape the outer edges of the pan with a silicone spatula to bring the egg mixture into the center. Cook for 2 minutes, continuing to fold the egg mixture into the center of the pan, forming large, long curds. If eggs begin to cook too quickly, remove the pan from the heat and allow to finish cooking in the hot pan. The eggs should be light, fluffy, and still moist.

Serves 4

···2···

# PARTY
# STARTERS

SOMETIMES, I HAVE LAUGHINGLY BEEN DESCRIBED as running on "Miller time." Everything always seems to take longer to put together than I expect. I definitely feel this was true in the last seconds of plating in the semifinals of *MasterChef.* In the nick of time, I creatively used the mixing bowl to pour on my hollandaise sauce. When I'm entertaining at home, my saving grace is to quickly assemble and serve appetizers. They keep my guests happy and give me time to put last-minute finishing touches on dinner.

Butter Bean Hummus
• 18 •

Collard Green Dip
• 21 •

Quick and Easy Cornbread Crostini
• 22 •

Cream Cheese Ring with Cranberry Chipotle Sauce
• 23 •

Bacon-Wrapped Stuffed Brussels Sprouts
• 26 •

BBQ Shrimp
• 28 •

Fingerling Potato Skins
• 29 •

Zucchini Cups
• 30 •

Crawfish Étouffée Rice Balls
• 32 •

Crab Cakes with Sweet and Spicy Coleslaw
• 35 •

White Pizza with Fried Sage
• 36 •

# Butter Bean Hummus

Butter beans are a staple ingredient in Southern cooking. When my mom was a little girl, she used to spend long, relaxing afternoons sitting on the porch shelling butter beans for her mother's recipes. This fast and easy appetizer uses canned butter beans so you don't have to shell for hours on end!

3 bacon strips

2 cans (15 ounces each) large butter beans, rinsed and drained

1 tablespoon fresh lemon juice (optional)

1 tablespoon tahini (optional)

1 teaspoon chopped fresh thyme leaves

1 small garlic clove, minced

Salt and ground black pepper

2 tablespoons extra-virgin olive oil

1 teaspoon thinly sliced scallion

¼ teaspoon paprika

Cook the bacon in a large skillet over low heat until crisp. Drain the bacon on paper towels (leave the bacon fat in the skillet). Break the bacon into small pieces and set aside.

Add the butter beans to the skillet and cook over medium heat for 5 minutes. Scrape the butter beans into a food processor and puree for 1 minute. Add 2 tablespoons water, the lemon juice (if using), tahini (if using), and thyme and process until smooth. Scrape the mixture into a bowl and stir in the garlic. Season to taste with salt and pepper.

To serve, transfer the bean mixture to a small serving bowl and smooth with the back of a spoon. Drizzle the olive oil over the hummus. Sprinkle with the bacon, scallion, and paprika. Serve with pita chips or fresh crudités.

Serves 4 to 6

# Collard Green Dip

In the South, collard greens are an abundant, but not well-respected green. This recipe takes lowly collards and elevates them in a delicious and creamy dip that can be served with Quick and Easy Cornbread Crostini, pita chips, or corn chips.

1 bunch (14 leaves) collard greens, washed and ribs removed

4 tablespoons ($\frac{1}{2}$ stick) unsalted butter

3 tablespoons diced yellow onion

2 garlic cloves, minced

$\frac{1}{4}$ cup all-purpose flour

$\frac{1}{4}$ cup reduced-sodium chicken broth

2 cups half-and-half

$\frac{1}{2}$ cup shredded Parmesan cheese (2 ounces)

$\frac{1}{2}$ tablespoon fresh lemon juice

$\frac{3}{8}$ teaspoon salt

$\frac{1}{8}$ teaspoon cayenne pepper

3 tablespoons sour cream

1 jar (6 ounces) marinated artichoke hearts, drained and chopped

$\frac{1}{4}$ cup shredded whole-milk mozzarella cheese or 1 ounce mozzarella, cut into 4 slices

Quick and Easy Cornbread Crostini (page 22) or pita chips

Bring a large pot of salted water to a boil over high heat. Add the collard greens and cook for 2 minutes to blanch. Drain the leaves and pat dry with paper towels. Stack the leaves and roll into a cigar. Cut the cigar in half lengthwise and thinly slice crosswise into long strips.

Preheat the oven to 350°F.

Melt the butter in a medium saucepan over low heat. Add the onion and cook until softened, about 4 minutes. Add the garlic and cook until fragrant, about 2 minutes. Sprinkle with the flour and cook for 1 minute. Whisk in the broth and half-and-half, increase the heat to medium and cook, stirring occasionally, for 5 minutes. Reduce the heat to low. Add the Parmesan, lemon juice, salt, and cayenne. Stir until the cheese has melted.

Pour the cheese mixture into a food processor and add the slivered greens. Blend or pulse until the greens are in small pieces. Return the mixture to the saucepan and cook for 5 minutes to heat through. Remove from the heat and stir in the sour cream and artichokes.

Pour the mixture into an 8 × 8-inch glass baking dish. Top with the mozzarella. Bake until the cheese is melted, about 10 minutes. Serve hot with cornbread crostini or pita chips.

Serves 8

# Quick and Easy Cornbread Crostini

Because I'm always entertaining for friends and family, I like to be able to whip up an appetizer quickly and easily when guests show up. I can make these cornbread crostini with ingredients I already have on hand in my pantry. They're so versatile—you can top them with anything from cheese (try spicy Pimiento Cheese, page 163) to salsa, and they're the perfect accompaniment to recipes like Collard Green Dip (page 21).

1 cup self-rising cornmeal
½ cup fat-free milk
1 large egg
2 tablespoons canola oil
¼ cup corn kernels

Preheat the oven to 450°F.

Mix together the cornmeal, milk, egg, oil, and corn in a medium bowl.

Heat a 24-cup mini muffin tin in the oven for 2 minutes. Once hot, lightly coat the cups with cooking spray.

Spoon ½ teaspoon of cornmeal mixture into each muffin cup. Bake for 5 minutes. Remove from the oven. Flip the crostini over using a spoon. Return to the oven and bake for 2 minutes to give an even crunch.

Makes about 48 crostini

# Cream Cheese Ring
# with Cranberry Chipotle Sauce

Cheese molds were a popular party appetizer back in the '50s, though they've all but disappeared now that cheese plates have become fashionable. This recipe brings an old-fashioned tradition into the 21st century with the addition of a sophisticated sauce and toasted walnuts. The presentation is simple and elegant and its vibrant red color makes it especially pretty to serve around the holidays.

### CRANBERRY CHIPOTLE SAUCE

1 bag (12 ounces) fresh cranberries

1½ cups granulated sugar

½ cup packed light brown sugar

1 tablespoon apple cider vinegar

1 chipotle pepper in adobo sauce

¼ teaspoon salt

1 tablespoon cornstarch

### CREAM CHEESE RING

1½ cups chopped walnuts

5 packages (8 ounces each) cream cheese, at room temperature

Crackers, for serving

To make the cranberry chipotle sauce: Combine the cranberries, both sugars, and 2 cups water in a large saucepan. Bring to a boil over medium-high heat. Reduce the heat to medium and cook for 20 minutes.

Strain half of the mixture into blender, reserving the pulp in the sieve. Add all of the remaining mixture to the blender without straining. (Transfer the reserved pulp back to the saucepan.) Add the vinegar, chipotle pepper, and salt to the blender and blend until smooth. Pour into the pan with the reserved pulp and stir to combine.

Stir 1 tablespoon water into the cornstarch in a small bowl. Stir the cornstarch mixture into the cranberry mixture until combined. Return the pan to medium heat and cook, stirring occasionally, until the mixture thickens, about 5 minutes.

Pour the sauce into a bowl and refrigerate for at least 2 hours or overnight before serving.

To prepare the cream cheese ring: Preheat the oven to 350°F. Spread the walnuts evenly on a baking sheet and bake, stirring occasionally, until fragrant and lightly toasted, 8 to 10 minutes.

Line a 7- or 8-inch springform pan with plastic wrap, leaving some hanging over the edges of the pan. Place 3 blocks of cream cheese in the bottom of the pan. Using your hand or the back of a spoon, spread the cream cheese evenly into the pan, making sure to get into the edges of the pan. Place a 6- or 8-ounce ramekin on top of the cream cheese, centered in the middle of the pan. Spread 2 blocks of cream

*(continued on page 24)*

cheese around the outside of the ramekin. Cover with plastic wrap. Refrigerate for 2 hours or until the cream cheese is firm. This can be made ahead of time and refrigerated overnight.

Release the sides of the springform and move the cream cheese ring off the bottom of the pan. Discard the plastic wrap and place the ring on a serving plate. Press the walnuts into the sides of the ring. Spoon some of the Cranberry Chipotle Sauce into the ramekin (and replenish as needed).

Serve with crackers.

Serves 12

Create a theme for your next entertaining event. For Southern charm, use a mixture of mason jars, tin or pewter serving pieces, and white dishes. Be sure to set the mood with flowers. White or yellow daisies work well and can be combined with curly willow sticks to lend height to the arrangement.

# Bacon-Wrapped Stuffed Brussels Sprouts

Brussels sprouts may seem like an unlikely choice for an appetizer, but the addition of bacon and cream cheese creates true Southern comfort that melts in your mouth with an explosion of flavor.

18 large Brussels sprouts, stem ends trimmed and loose outer leaves discarded

4 ounces cream cheese or goat cheese, at room temperature

1/2 teaspoon minced garlic

9 bacon slices, halved crosswise

2 tablespoons extra-virgin olive oil

1/8 teaspoon ground black pepper

Fill a large pot halfway with water and bring to a boil over high heat. Add the Brussels sprouts and cook for 2 minutes to blanch. Remove with a slotted spoon and drain in a sieve. Pat the Brussels sprouts dry with paper towels or a kitchen towel. Using a paring knife, cut an "X" in the top of each Brussels sprout, cutting halfway down through the sprout.

Preheat the oven to 400°F.

Blend the cheese and garlic in a small bowl. Spoon the cheese mixture into a small resealable plastic bag. Cut a small hole in one of the bottom corners of the bag. Place the cut-out corner of the plastic bag in the "X" of each Brussels sprout and squeeze in a dollop of cheese mixture.

Wrap a piece of bacon around each sprout vertically, covering over the cheese. Place on a rimmed baking sheet. Drizzle the oil over the sprouts and sprinkle with the pepper.

Bake the sprouts, flipping them over halfway through the baking time, until the bacon is evenly browned, 25 to 30 minutes. Serve with toothpicks.

Serves 9

# BBQ Shrimp

BBQ shrimp are commonly served in New Orleans restaurants with their heads and tails still on. I have made the eating easier and more "dignified" by using peeled shrimp. However, you may still catch me sopping up the sauce with French bread (in the most elegant way, of course)!

8 tablespoons (1 stick) unsalted butter

3/4 cup chicken broth

1/4 cup Worcestershire sauce

1 tablespoon soy sauce

1 1/2 teaspoons fresh lemon juice

1 garlic clove, minced

3/8 teaspoon onion powder

1/4 teaspoon cracked black pepper

1/8 teaspoon paprika

Pinch of cayenne pepper

1 pound large shrimp, peeled and deveined

Combine all the ingredients except the shrimp in a cast-iron skillet over medium-high heat. Cook until the mixture has reduced and thickened slightly, 4 to 6 minutes.

Add the shrimp and cook until just barely opaque throughout, about 3 minutes. Serve hot.

Serves 4

When I was growing up, everyone had a part in preparing our family meals. Start this tradition in your family. Make meal times fun by giving each family member a task in the meal preparation, even if it's simply buttering bread—it's a great way to learn how to cook!

# Fingerling Potato Skins

My dad is a big sports fan, so our family often hosts parties on game days. Potato skins are the perfect snack or appetizer to munch on while watching the big game. My version, which uses fingerling potatoes, creates smaller, more elegant "skins," making them just as suitable for serving as an elegant appetizer.

1 pound fingerling potatoes (18 to 20 potatoes)

1 tablespoon extra-virgin olive oil

1/2 teaspoon kosher salt

Pimiento Cheese (page 163)

Preheat the oven to 400°F.

Place the potatoes on a rimmed baking sheet. Toss them with the oil and salt. Bake for 30 minutes. Let cool slightly. (Leave the oven on.)

Halve the potatoes lengthwise. Remove most of the pulp, leaving a little in the bottom to give the skins structure (I use a metal 1/4-teaspoon measuring spoon for this.) Mash 1/2 cup of the pulp (you can reserve the rest for another recipe). Combine the mashed potato pulp with the spicy Pimiento Cheese.

Place the potatoes skin-side up on the baking sheet. Bake for 6 to 10 minutes. Turn the potatoes over and spoon 2 to 3 teaspoons cheese-potato mixture into the skins. Bake until the cheese is bubbling, 3 to 4 minutes. Serve hot.

Serves 8 to 10

# Zucchini Cups

Hospitality in the South is not only expressed through hosting and entertaining, but also through generous giving. It's not unusual to find a bag of freshly picked zucchini on your doorstep in the summertime left by a neighbor with a bumper crop. I'm always experimenting with new and creative ways to use this overabundant vegetable—and this appetizer recipe is one of my favorites.

4 medium zucchini

1 tablespoon extra-virgin olive oil

$\frac{1}{8}$ teaspoon salt

$\frac{1}{8}$ teaspoon ground black pepper

$1\frac{1}{4}$ cups reduced-sodium chicken broth

$\frac{1}{4}$ cup diced yellow onion

$2\frac{1}{2}$ tablespoons unsalted butter

$\frac{1}{2}$ teaspoon crushed garlic

$\frac{1}{8}$ teaspoon ground white pepper

1 large egg, beaten

3 tablespoons Italian-style breadcrumbs

1 tablespoon grated Parmesan cheese

Preheat the oven to 375°F.

Slice off the bottom, rounded end of each zucchini so that it will stand up on the baking sheet. Measure 3 inches up from the bottom and cut crosswise into 4 pieces (for a total of 16). Reserve the remaining pieces of zucchini (the stem ends). Using a melon baller or $\frac{1}{2}$-teaspoon measuring spoon, scoop the pulp from the zucchini pieces to make "cups," leaving a thin layer of zucchini at the bottom of each cup. (Reserve the pulp for another use.)

Place the zucchini cups on a baking sheet. Coat the outside of the cups with the oil. Season with salt and black pepper. Bake for 17 minutes. Remove from the oven and reduce the temperature to 350°F.

Meanwhile, in a medium saucepan, bring the broth to a boil over medium-high heat. Peel the reserved zucchini tops and trim off the stem ends. Cut the zucchini into 1-inch cubes and measure out about $2\frac{1}{2}$ cups. Add the zucchini cubes and onion to the boiling broth. Cook until the zucchini is soft, about 8 minutes.

Drain the zucchini mixture and return the vegetables to the pan. Using a potato masher, mash the zucchini-onion mixture. Add 1 tablespoon of the butter, the garlic, and white pepper. Stir until combined. Stir in the egg. Fill the zucchini cups with the zucchini mixture. Bake until the mixture is set, about 15 minutes.

Meanwhile, melt the remaining $1\frac{1}{2}$ tablespoons butter in a small skillet over medium heat. Stir in the breadcrumbs and cook for 1 minute. Remove from the heat and stir in the Parmesan.

Spoon a heaping teaspoon on top of each zucchini cup. Bake until the breading is golden brown, about 15 minutes. Serve hot.

Serves 8

# Crawfish Étouffée Rice Balls

Rice balls are a trendy menu item in contemporary restaurants, but here in the South, *calas*, or fried rice balls, have been eaten for centuries. The word *calas* means fried rice cake or fritter. It comes from the African word for rice. Rice balls were sold on the street corners in New Orleans as early as the 1800s. This recipe is my version of a spicy "rice ball."

1 tablespoon unsalted butter

½ cup diced yellow onion

½ cup diced celery

½ cup diced red bell pepper

1 teaspoon minced garlic

1¾ cups chicken broth

6 ounces peeled crawfish tails or shrimp, chopped

⅛ teaspoon salt

¼ teaspoon ground black pepper

Pinch of cayenne pepper

1 large egg

2 large egg whites

3 cups cooked jasmine rice

1 tablespoon all purpose flour

10 cubes (½ inch) mozzarella cheese

3 tablespoons canola oil

3 cups panko breadcrumbs

2 teaspoons rice flour

1 tablespoon sliced scallions (optional)

Melt the butter in a medium cast-iron skillet over medium heat. Add the onion, celery, and bell pepper. Cook, stirring occasionally, over medium heat until the vegetables are softened, about 10 minutes. Add the garlic and cook until fragrant, about 2 minutes.

Stir in 1 cup of the broth and simmer over medium heat for 5 minutes. Add the crawfish (or shrimp) and cook until just opaque, 1 to 2 minutes.

Drain the mixture in a sieve set over a medium bowl. Return the liquid to the skillet and scoop the crawfish mixture (in the sieve) into the medium bowl. Season the crawfish mixture with the salt, ⅛ teaspoon of the black pepper, and the cayenne. Set aside to cool at room temperature.

Beat together the whole egg and egg whites. When the crawfish mixture is cooled, stir in the beaten eggs, rice, and flour.

Line a baking sheet with plastic wrap. Measure out ¼ cup of the rice mixture and put it in the palm of your hand. Place a cheese cube in the center of the rice mixture. Gently form into a ball around the cheese. Place on the baking sheet. Repeat the process to make a total of 10 rice balls. Refrigerate for at least 15 minutes.

Preheat the oven to 400°F.

Heat the oil in a small skillet over medium-high heat. Spread the panko in a plate. Working with 1 rice ball at a time, pat the panko crumbs around the ball. Gently press the ball in your palms to keep a compact sphere shape. Carefully place 2 rice balls in the hot oil. Turn the balls with a fork, browning them all over. Repeat with the remaining balls.

When all rice balls have been browned, place them on a baking sheet. Bake for 8 to 10 minutes. Transfer the rice balls to a paper towel–lined plate to cool slightly.

While the rice balls are baking, make the sauce. Whisk together the rice flour and remaining ¾ cup broth in a small saucepan. Cook over medium-high heat, stirring constantly, until thickened, about 8 minutes. Reduce the heat to a simmer and keep hot until ready to serve.

To serve, spoon a large spoonful of sauce on a small plate. Place a rice ball on the sauce. If desired, sprinkle scallions on top.

Serves 10

A well-stocked pantry is important for entertaining unexpected guests. With a few basic ingredients and creativity, it is easy to whip up an appetizer or dessert. My Quick and Easy Cornbread Crostini can be made with basic ingredients such as eggs, milk, and cornmeal.

# Crab Cakes with Sweet and Spicy Coleslaw

Living close to the Mississippi and Louisiana coastal waters, I grew up going on fishing expeditions with my dad. My mother's family also had a fishing camp at La Frances in Bay St. Louis, Mississippi, where we used to catch fish, crabs, and shrimp. My family has had the opportunity to enjoy a lot of fresh, delicious seafood over the years—and we've perfected the art of the crab cake!

2 large eggs

4 tablespoons mayonnaise

1/4 teaspoon grated lemon zest

2 tablespoons fresh lemon juice

1 teaspoon spicy mustard

2 tablespoons grated yellow onion

2 tablespoons chopped chives

1/4 teaspoon black pepper blend

1/8 teaspoon ground coriander

Pinch of cayenne pepper

1/4 teaspoon salt

1 pound fresh jumbo lump crab meat

1 cup panko breadcrumbs

4 tablespoons (1/2 stick) unsalted butter

1/4 cup canola oil

Sweet and Spicy Coleslaw (page 78)

Lightly beat the eggs in a large bowl. Whisk in the mayonnaise, lemon zest, lemon juice, mustard, onion, chives, black pepper blend, coriander, cayenne, and salt.

Gently fold in the crab meat and 1/2 cup of the panko.

Cover a baking sheet with plastic wrap. Using a 1/4-cup measuring cup, scoop out crab meat mixture and form cakes with your hands, for a total of 12 crab cakes; place them on the baking sheet as you work. Cover loosely with plastic wrap and chill in refrigerator for 30 minutes.

Place the remaining 1/2 cup panko on a plate. One at a time, gently place the chilled crab cakes in the panko, pressing the crumbs onto the cakes and coating both sides.

Heat a 12-inch cast iron skillet over medium-high heat. Add the butter and oil. When hot, place 6 crab cakes in the skillet. Cook until lightly browned and crispy, about 3 minutes on each side. Drain on a paper towel–lined plate. Repeat with the remaining 6 crab cakes.

Serve with Sweet and Spicy Coleslaw.

Makes 12 crab cakes

# White Pizza with Fried Sage

While the art of frying food is certainly a longstanding Southern tradition, frying fresh herbs is a more recent culinary trend that's become popular in restaurants across the country. Here, aromatic fried sage leaves provide the perfect flavor and texture to balance the earthiness of fresh Parmesan, garlic, and mushrooms. You can cut the pizza into small squares to serve as an appetizer or cut larger wedges if serving as an entrée.

## DOUGH

1 envelope (1/4 ounce) active dry yeast

1 2/3 cups lukewarm (100° to 110°F) water

4 cups plus 3 tablespoons bread flour

1/4 cup plus 3 tablespoons extra-virgin olive oil

2 1/2 teaspoons salt

1 tablespoon yellow cornmeal

## SAUCE

1 tablespoon unsalted butter

1 tablespoon all-purpose flour

1 cup heavy cream

2 small garlic cloves, minced

1 tablespoon grated Parmesan cheese

1/4 teaspoon salt

## TOPPING

6 baby bella mushrooms, thinly sliced

6 slices fresh mozzarella cheese (about 1 1/2 ounces)

8 fresh sage leaves

To make the dough: In a stand mixer, whisk together the yeast and lukewarm water. Let stand for 5 minutes. Add the 4 cups bread flour, 1/4 cup of the oil, and the salt. Using a paddle attachment, beat on medium speed until the dough is smooth. Replace the paddle with the dough hook and increase the speed to high. After about 2 minutes, the dough should form and be sticky.

Sprinkle 3 tablespoons bread flour onto clean surface. Turn the dough out onto the surface and knead in the flour. Form the dough into a smooth ball, adding a little more flour if the dough is too sticky. Place the dough in a lightly oiled bowl and turn to coat. Cover the bowl with plastic wrap and let rise for 1 hour or until doubled in size.

Meanwhile, to make the sauce: Melt the butter in a medium skillet over medium heat. Stir in the all-purpose flour and cook for 1 minute. Whisking constantly, slowly pour in the cream. Simmer, whisking, for 3 minutes. Stir in the garlic, Parmesan, and salt. Reduce the heat to low and cook, stirring, until the cheese melts, about 3 minutes. Set the sauce aside.

Place an oven rack in the bottom position and preheat to 450·F. About 10 minutes before the dough has doubled in size, put a pizza stone on the bottom rack to preheat.

Punch the dough down and divide in half. (Wrap one half of the dough and save for another use.) Place the remaining half of the dough on a floured surface. Using a rolling pin, roll out into a round large enough to cover the pizza stone. Remove the stone from the oven and sprinkle with the cornmeal. Carefully place the dough on the stone. Poke a few holes into the dough with a fork. Bake until risen but not browned, about 5 minutes. Remove the crust from the oven and spread the sauce over the dough. Arrange mushrooms and mozzarella over the sauce. Bake until cheese is melted and bubbling, 10 to 15 minutes.

Meanwhile, heat the remaining 3 tablespoons oil in a small skillet over medium-high heat. When the oil is hot, fry the sage leaves 2 at a time in the oil until crispy but not browned, about 20 seconds. Remove the leaves and drain on a paper towel.

Remove the pizza from the oven and arrange the fried sage leaves on top. Slice with a pizza cutter into small squares and place on a serving platter. Serve hot.

Serves 8

**Recipe Name** _Onion Soup_

Ingredients & Directions

Microwave for 9 min. 2 small
onions sliced + 2 tbls. butter
Stir in 2 teasp. flour and
microwave. 1 min.
Add 2 cans beef broth, 2 tbls.
Madeira and 1 tsp. Worchestershire
Microwave for 6-8 min.

Add
French bread- sprinkle garlic
salt, parmesian, ¼ cup mozzarella,
Cheddar- Microwave 45 sec.

---

**Recipe Name** _Broccoli Soup_

Ingredients & Directions

3 cups broccoli (10-oz)

1 cup chicken broth

____ tsp. onion          boil

¼ tsp. ____ pepper

Simmer 8-___ min. Blend,
Add 3 ¼ cup ____.
Stir cornstarch into ¼ tsp.
milk and add.
Stir in 6-oz. velve___.

PAGE

# 3

## SOUPS, SALADS, AND SANDWICHES

ALTHOUGH WINTER IS SHORT in the South, my family and I relish every minute of it. On our 7 acres of wooded land, some of our most memorable entertaining experiences have included crackling bonfires with long wire skewers of toasty marshmallow desserts dangling over the flames. I love warming everyone up with a variety of soups, whether it is my rich and meaty Game-Day Chili or the light and creamy Roasted Eggplant Soup.

# Southern Zuppa

*Zuppa* is the Italian word for soup. This recipe was inspired by a soup I enjoyed at an Italian restaurant, which featured potatoes, white beans, kale, and sausage. By using Southern and Cajun ingredients, I transformed this Italian soup into a soulful Southern dish. I like to cook a whole chicken when I make this soup, even though you won't need to use all of the meat for this recipe. It's always handy to have leftover chicken on hand for a quick meal. Try using yours in my Lemon-Pepper Chicken Salad (page 50).

1 whole chicken (about 5 pounds)

1 carrot, coarsely chopped

Salt

3 collard green leaves, ribs removed, rolled into cigar, halved, and cut into ½-inch strips

2 cups cubed red potatoes

1 cup sliced (½ inch) cooked fresh andouille sausage

1 can (16 ounces) large butter beans or lima beans, rinsed and drained

¼ cup diced yellow onion

1 garlic clove, minced

Ground black pepper

2 tablespoons heavy cream

¼ cup shredded Parmesan cheese

Combine the chicken and water to cover (about 10 cups) in a large pot. Add the carrot and 1 teaspoon salt. Bring to a boil. Reduce to a simmer, cover tightly, and cook until a thermometer inserted in the thickest part of a thigh registers 165°F, about 1 hour, skimming off any foam that rises to the surface.

Meanwhile, stack the collard leaves, roll them into a cigar, halve it lengthwise, and cut crosswise into ½-inch-wide strips.

Remove the cooked chicken from the broth and let cool. When cool enough to handle, pull the chicken meat from the bones. Shred into pieces with two forks. Measure out 1 cup of mixed light and dark meat for the soup. (Reserve the remainder for another use.)

Strain the broth into a bowl and discard the fat. Return the strained broth to the pot and bring to a simmer. Add the potatoes, sausage, beans, collards, onion, garlic, and ½ teaspoon salt. Gently simmer, covered, for 20 minutes.

Add the chicken meat and cream to the soup. Simmer until the chicken is heated through, 5 to 7 minutes. Taste for seasoning and add more salt and pepper if desired.

Ladle into bowls and top with Parmesan.

Serves 4 to 6

# Roasted Eggplant Soup
# with Sun-Dried Tomato Cream

In summertime it seems like everyone struggles with what to do with all of the eggplants their gardens produce. My roasted eggplant soup is a great way to use up this bountiful vegetable and makes an elegant start to any meal.

## SOUP

2 large eggplants, halved lengthwise

2 tablespoons extra-virgin olive oil

1 teaspoon kosher salt

6 small garlic cloves, unpeeled

2 tablespoons unsalted butter

$^2/_3$ cup diced yellow onion

2 cups reduced-sodium chicken broth

1 cup heavy cream

$^1/_2$ teaspoon ground white pepper

## SUN-DRIED TOMATO CREAM

1 cup heavy cream, cold

2 oil-packed sun-dried tomatoes, drained and finely diced

## CROUTONS AND GARNISH

1 cup cubed ($^1/_2$ inch) Rosemary Focaccia (page 81)

1 tablespoon extra-virgin olive oil

$^1/_8$ teaspoon garlic salt

$^1/_4$ cup crumbled Gorgonzola cheese

Preheat the oven to 400°F. To make the soup: Score the skin of the eggplant with a knife, making several small slits. Coat the eggplant with the oil and kosher salt on both sides and place skin-side up on a baking sheet. Wrap the garlic in foil and place on baking sheet. Bake until the eggplant is softened, about 30 minutes. Remove from the oven and flip the eggplant cut-side up. Carefully remove and discard the seeds from the eggplant. Spoon the pulp into a bowl. Set the garlic aside.

In a medium saucepan, melt the butter over medium-low heat. Add the onion and cook until translucent, 3 to 5 minutes. Squeeze the garlic out of the skin and add to the pan. Scrape the eggplant pulp into the pan and cook over low heat for 15 minutes to blend the flavors.

Add the broth and bring to a boil. Reduce to a simmer and cook for 20 minutes. Strain through a fine-mesh sieve into a medium bowl. Pour the strained mixture back into the pot and stir in the cream and white pepper. Simmer over low heat, stirring occasionally, for 20 minutes.

To make the sun-dried tomato cream: Process the cream and sun-dried tomatoes in a food processor until smooth. Pour into a chilled mixing bowl. Using an electric mixer, beat until soft peaks form.

To make the croutons: Preheat the oven to 400°F. Coat a baking sheet with cooking spray. Spread the focaccia cubes on the baking sheet and bake until lightly toasted, 8 to 10 minutes. Heat the oil in a medium skillet over medium-high heat. Toss the focaccia cubes with the garlic salt in a bowl. Add the cubes to the pan and cook until the bread cubes are lightly browned and fragrant, 2 to 3 minutes.

Ladle the soup into bowls and top with a dollop of sun-dried tomato cream, the focaccia croutons, and Gorgonzola crumbles.

Serves 4

# Loaded Cauliflower Soup

This hearty soup was inspired by the idea of baked potato soup. Roasting the cauliflower imparts a rich, earthy flavor that adds depth to the soup. The classic baked potato toppings such as cheese, sour cream, and scallions "load" it with flavor.

8 cups cauliflower florets (from 1 head)

2 tablespoons extra-virgin olive oil

Kosher salt

1 tablespoon unsalted butter

1/4 cup diced yellow onion

1 garlic clove, minced

2 cups reduced-sodium chicken broth

1 1/2 cups heavy cream

1/2 cup half-and-half

2 teaspoons chopped fresh tarragon

1/8 teaspoon ground white pepper

GARNISH

1/4 cup shredded sharp Cheddar cheese

1/4 cup sour cream

2 tablespoons chopped scallions

Preheat oven to 400°F.

Toss the cauliflower with the oil on a baking sheet. Sprinkle the florets with 1/2 teaspoon salt. Roast until the cauliflower is fork-tender and lightly browned in spots, about 25 minutes.

Meanwhile, melt the butter in a large saucepan over medium heat. Add the onion and cook until translucent, about 4 minutes. Add the garlic and cook for 1 minute, making sure the garlic doesn't brown.

Add all but 1/2 cup of the roasted cauliflower florets to the saucepan. Add 1 cup of the broth and 1/2 cup of the cream. Cook over medium heat for 5 minutes.

Working in batches, transfer the mixture to a blender and blend until smooth. Return the puree to the saucepan. Stir in the half-and-half and the remaining 1 cup cream and 1 cup broth. Simmer over medium heat for 25 minutes to blend the flavors.

Chop of the reserved 1/2 cup cauliflower and stir into the soup. Simmer for 5 more minutes to heat through. Stir in the tarragon and white pepper. Season with salt to taste.

Ladle the soup into 4 bowls and top each serving with Cheddar, sour cream, and scallions.

Serves 4

# Game-Day Chili

Who doesn't love a homemade bowl of warming, stick-to-your ribs chili? I like to make this recipe on a Saturday or Sunday during football season when the air turns crisp. A big pot of chili makes for a great tailgating menu item. When serving it at home. I like to set out little bowls of toppings so my guests can make their own creations.

## CHILI

3 tablespoons canola oil

1 pound beef stew meat, cut into 1-inch cubes

4 tablespoons all-purpose flour

2 cups reduced-sodium beef stock

2 tablespoons extra-virgin olive oil

½ green bell pepper, diced

½ small onion, diced

1 tablespoon chili powder

1½ teaspoons ground cumin

5 garlic cloves, minced

1 pound ground beef

1 can (15 ounces) kidney beans, rinsed and drained

1 can (15 ounces) black beans, rinsed and drained

1 can (14.5 ounces) diced tomatoes

3 chipotle peppers in adobe sauce, thinly sliced

## TOPPINGS

1 cup shredded Cheddar cheese

1 bunch scallions, thinly sliced

1 container (16 ounces) sour cream

1 cup coarsely chopped fresh cilantro (optional)

To make the chili: Heat the canola oil in a large soup pot over medium-low heat. Dredge the meat in 2 tablespoons of the flour. Add to the pot and brown on all sides, about 5 minutes. Add the stock and simmer until the beef is almost tender but not falling apart, about 30 minutes.

Meanwhile, heat the olive oil in a large skillet over medium-low heat. Add the bell pepper and onion and cook until softened, about 4 minutes. Add the chili powder, cumin, and garlic and cook 1 minute longer. Add the ground beef to the pan and cook, breaking up the meat with a wooden spoon, until cooked through, about 7 minutes. Spoon the fat from the pan and discard.

When the stew meat has cooked for 30 minutes, add the ground beef and vegetables. Add both beans, the diced tomatoes, and the chipotle peppers. Gently simmer on low heat for 45 minutes to meld the flavors. Stir occasionally to make sure the chili doesn't stick to the bottom of the pot.

Meanwhile, to prepare the toppings: Place all of the toppings in individual bowls to pass at the table.

Ladle the chili into bowls or mugs and serve with the toppings.

Serves 6

# Blackened Catfish Salad with Cornbread Croutons

Because catfish are plentiful in the coastal waters of Mississippi, I like to use them as often as possible in my fish dishes. Catfish is not only an economical choice, it's also a versatile one—its mild flavor lends it to a variety of uses. Its flaky texture also makes it the perfect choice for fish tacos and salads such as this one.

**ROASTED CORN**

1 ear corn, unhusked

1 tablespoon unsalted butter, at room temperature

⅛ teaspoon salt

⅛ teaspoon ground black pepper

**CROUTONS**

1 cup cubed (½ inch) Jalapeño Cornbread (page 83)

⅛ teaspoon onion powder

⅛ teaspoon dried chives

Pinch of salt

¾ teaspoon extra-virgin olive oil

**FISH**

4 catfish fillets (about 5 ounces each)

1 teaspoon fresh lemon juice

1½ teaspoons Blackened Seasoning Rub (page 158)

1 tablespoon extra-virgin olive oil

**SALAD**

6 cups mixed greens

Dressing from Dillicious Potato Salad (page 70)

½ cup halved grape tomatoes

¼ cup shredded sharp Cheddar cheese

Preheat the oven to 400°F.

To prepare the corn: Peel the husk back, remove the silk, rub the cob with 1 tablespoon butter, and sprinkle with the salt and pepper. Replace the husk and place on a baking sheet. Bake until lightly browned, about 20 minutes. When cool enough to handle, cut the kernels off the cob into a small bowl.

To make the croutons: Coat a baking sheet with cooking spray. In a small bowl, toss the cornbread cubes, onion powder, chives, and salt. Spread on the baking sheet and bake until lightly toasted, about 12 minutes.

Heat a medium skillet over medium-high heat. Add the oil. Add the cornbread cubes and cook for 2 to 3 minutes, tossing occasionally in pan. Remove and let cool slightly.

To prepare the fish: Place the fillets on a plate and sprinkle with the lemon juice. Sprinkle the blackened seasoning over one side of the fillets.

Heat a grill pan over medium heat and brush with the oil. Place the fillets seasoned-side down on the pan. Cook until the fish flakes easily with a fork, 5 to 6 minutes per side. Transfer to a plate.

To assemble the salads: Place the greens in a bowl and toss with just enough dressing to barely coat the leaves. Divide the dressed mixed greens among 4 plates. Top each with some roasted corn, grape tomatoes, and cheese. Lay the catfish fillets on top of the salads. Top with the croutons. Serve with extra dressing on the side.

Serves 4

# Lemon-Pepper Chicken Salad

This fresh and easy approach to chicken salad is so versatile—you can dress it up or down. Serve it on sandwich bread for an outdoor lunch or picnic; use Boston Bibb lettuce to create wraps for a ladies' lunch or spa day; or for a special occasion, try serving it in savory profiteroles.

¾ pound boneless, skinless chicken breasts

2½ teaspoons plus 1 tablespoon fresh lemon juice

2 teaspoons lemon-pepper seasoning

1 teaspoon kosher salt

1 tablespoon water

6 tablespoons mayonnaise

1 hard-boiled egg, chopped

¼ cup diced Granny Smith apple

1½ tablespoons dried cranberries

1½ tablespoons chopped pecans, toasted

Preheat the oven to 350°F.

Place the chicken breast in a glass baking dish. Sprinkle 2½ teaspoons of the lemon juice over the chicken. Sprinkle with the lemon-pepper seasoning and salt. Add 1 tablespoon water to the bottom of the dish. Cover with foil and bake until the chicken is cooked through but still juicy (and a thermometer inserted in the thickest part registers 155°F), 45 to 50 minutes. Let cool.

When the chicken is cool enough to handle, shred it with 2 forks and place in a medium bowl. Stir in the mayonnaise and remaining 1 tablespoon lemon juice. Add the egg, apple, cranberries, and pecans. Stir until combined.

Serves 6

# Southern Cobb Salad

This colorful salad makes for a satisfying weekday lunch or dinner and can also be served as a side salad at a barbecue or picnic. While the presence of bacon, egg, cheese, and corn make it similar to a traditional Cobb salad, the addition of field peas and fresh buttermilk dressing give it a Southern twist.

1⅓ cups corn kernels, fresh or thawed frozen

1⅓ cups field peas or frozen black-eyed peas

3 cups chopped romaine lettuce

1 cup halved grape tomatoes

½ cup shredded Cheddar cheese (2 ounces)

½ cup chopped cooked bacon

2 hard-boiled eggs, chopped

Buttermilk Herb Dressing (page 160)

Preheat the oven to 400°F. Lightly coat a baking sheet with cooking spray. Spread the corn on the baking sheet and roast until the corn is lightly browned, about 10 minutes, flipping halfway through the cooking time. Set aside to cool.

Bring a small pot of water to a boil over high heat. Add the field peas (or black-eyed peas), reduce to a simmer, cover and cook for 10 minutes. Drain the peas and let cool.

On a large serving platter, arrange each ingredient in a neat pile and allow guests to assemble their own salads. Serve with the dressing on the side.

Serves 4

# Petite Shrimp Rolls

Living so close to the Gulf Coast has its advantages—and buying shrimp fresh off the boat is one of them. I don't like to add too much mayo to my shrimp rolls—I prefer to let the flavor of the shrimp shine through, enhanced with a little lemon juice and zest. These petite rolls are perfect for an afternoon tea or luncheon and are a lot less messy to eat than most traditional seafood "rolls."

1 pound medium shrimp, peeled and deveined

2 tablespoons mayonnaise

2 tablespoons chopped scallions

1 teaspoon grated lemon zest

1 teaspoon thinly sliced fresh chives

$\frac{1}{2}$ teaspoon fresh lemon juice

$\frac{1}{8}$ teaspoon salt

Pinch of ground black pepper

1 cup mixed salad greens (spinach, arugula, etc.)

8 petite rolls, split lengthwise

Coat a medium skillet with cooking spray and place over medium-high heat. Add the shrimp and cook until opaque throughout, about 7 minutes. Transfer the shrimp to a plate to cool for 5 minutes.

When cool enough to handle, chop the shrimp into small pieces. Transfer to a medium bowl and stir in the mayonnaise, scallions, lemon zest, chives, lemon juice, salt, and black pepper.

To assemble, place some greens on the bottom of each roll. Top with $\frac{1}{4}$ cup shrimp mixture and the top of the other half of the roll.

Serves 8

# Pulled Pork BBQ Sandwiches

My dad grew up in Memphis, Tennessee—a.k.a., barbecue country. Every time we make a family trip to Tennessee, we make it a mission to find the best pulled pork BBQ sandwich in the state. I wanted to re-create for my dad the taste of real Memphis BBQ, but with a special twist. I use my own blend of seasoning rub to roast the pork, then top it off with a traditional BBQ sauce at the end. Roasting the pork at a low temperature definitely takes time . . . but the end result is so tender and delicious, it's worth it.

### RUB

2 tablespoons chili powder

2 tablespoons garlic salt

1½ tablespoons paprika

1 tablespoon turbinado sugar

½ tablespoon ground cumin

¼ teaspoon dried parsley flakes

1 teaspoon black pepper blend

1 teaspoon unsweetened cocoa powder

### PORK

10 pounds boneless Boston butt or pork shoulder

1 large yellow onion, sliced

1 large jar (18 ounces) of your favorite BBQ sauce

15 sandwich buns

Preheat the oven to 400°F.

To make the rub: Combine all the rub ingredients in a small bowl.

To make the pork: Rub the pork all over with the rub. Place fat-side up on a rack in a roasting pan (The rack allows the pork fat to drip to the bottom of the pan.) Place the onion slices on top of the pork. Fill the bottom of the roasting pan with 2 inches of water.

Roast the pork for 1 hour. Reduce the heat to 250°F and roast until a thermometer inserted in the thickest part registers 160°F, about 10 hours, adding more water to the pan as it evaporates. When pork is cooked through, remove from the oven and let rest for at least 30 minutes. Cut any visible fat away from the pork and discard. Place the pork in a 4-quart baking dish. Using two forks, pull the pork meat into shreds.

Heat the BBQ sauce in a medium saucepan over medium heat. Once the sauce is warm, pour it over the pulled pork. Stir the meat and sauce together until the meat is coated in sauce.

Warm the buns on a baking sheet in the turned-off but still-warm oven for about 3 minutes.

Serve the pulled pork BBQ with warmed buns.

Makes 15 sandwiches

# Mississippi Cheesesteak

Food has always played a major part in the planning of our family vacations. We all enjoy seeking out new restaurants and embrace the challenge of finding the country's best versions of our favorite foods. My older sister, Leslie, was on a mission to find America's best cheesesteak. But after sampling what many states have to offer, this Mississippi Cheesesteak is still her favorite!

1 loaf crusty French bread

About 1 pound sliced leftover Grandma's Sunday Roast (page 110)

Sautéed onions, peppers, and/or mushrooms (optional)

½ cup spicy Pimiento Cheese (page 163)

Preheat the broiler.

Cut bread crosswise into 4 lengths and split each one lengthwise. Place both halves of the bread cut-side up on a baking sheet. Top one side of each sandwich with beef, vegetables (if using), and 2 tablespoons Pimiento Cheese. Broil until the cheese begins to melt and the bread is toasted. Top the sandwiches with other half of the bread and serve.

Serves 4

# Stuffed Muffuletta Po' Boys

The muffuletta sandwich originated in the early 1900s at Central Grocery in New Orleans. Traditional muffulettas contain salami, ham, cheese, and the absolutely essential ingredient of olive salad. Though you can buy jarred olive salad in the South, I prefer to make my own (see page 162). I like to make these sandwiches with pistolettes (another regional specialty), but if they're not available where you live, you can substitute unsliced mini-baguettes.

8 pistolettes (small football-shaped rolls)

4 tablespoons chopped pepperoni

4 tablespoons chopped Genoa salami

8 tablespoons Olive Salad (page 162)

8 tablespoons chopped cooked ham

16 cubes ($\frac{1}{2}$ inch) part-skim mozzarella cheese

4 tablespoons ($\frac{1}{2}$ stick) unsalted butter, melted

Preheat the oven to 375°F.

Cut a 1-inch hole at both ends of each pistolette. Using your fingers, hollow out the center of the pistolette. (Save the pistolette stuffing for fresh breadcrumbs or another use.)

Toss the pepperoni and salami together in a small bowl. Into each pistolette, spoon $\frac{1}{2}$ tablespoon olive salad, $\frac{1}{2}$ tablespoon ham, $\frac{1}{2}$ tablespoon pepperoni-salami mixture, and 1 cube cheese. Repeat the layering 3 more times.

Place the stuffed pistolettes on a baking sheet. Brush the melted butter over all sides of the pistolettes. Bake until rolls are hot and slightly toasted, 8 to 12 minutes. Serve warm.

Serves 4

# Off-the-Griddle Cheeseburger

Your quest for the perfect burger ends here! My Miracle Marinade (page 159) enhances the natural flavors of the ground meat and makes this burger moist and juicy. Top it off with spicy Pimento Cheese (page 163) and a little Sun-Dried Tomato and Cranberry Ketchup (page 161), and I dare you to find a more mouthwatering burger east or west of the Mississippi.

1 cup beef stock

¼ cup beef broth

¼ cup Miracle Marinade (page 159)

1½ pounds ground beef, preferably chuck

½ teaspoon salt

¼ teaspoon ground black pepper

⅓ cup spicy Pimiento Cheese (page 163)

6 hamburger buns

Sun-Dried Tomato and Cranberry Ketchup (optional; page 161)

Lettuce and tomato slices (optional)

Combine the beef stock, beef broth, and marinade in a small saucepan over medium heat. Gently simmer the mixture for 10 minutes. Reduce the heat to low and cook for 15 minutes to reduce. Transfer to a bowl to cool.

Combine the ground beef, salt, and pepper. Add 2 tablespoons of the cooled marinade mixture. Mix the ingredients until well combined. Form meat into 6 patties.

Heat a grill pan over medium heat. Coat the pan with cooking spray. Cook the patties to desired doneness, or 5 to 6 minutes on each side for medium-well. Top the burgers with equal amounts (1 scant tablespoon) of the Pimiento Cheese during the final 2 minutes of cooking.

Assemble the burgers on the buns and top with the cranberry ketchup and/or lettuce and tomato, if desired.

Serves 6

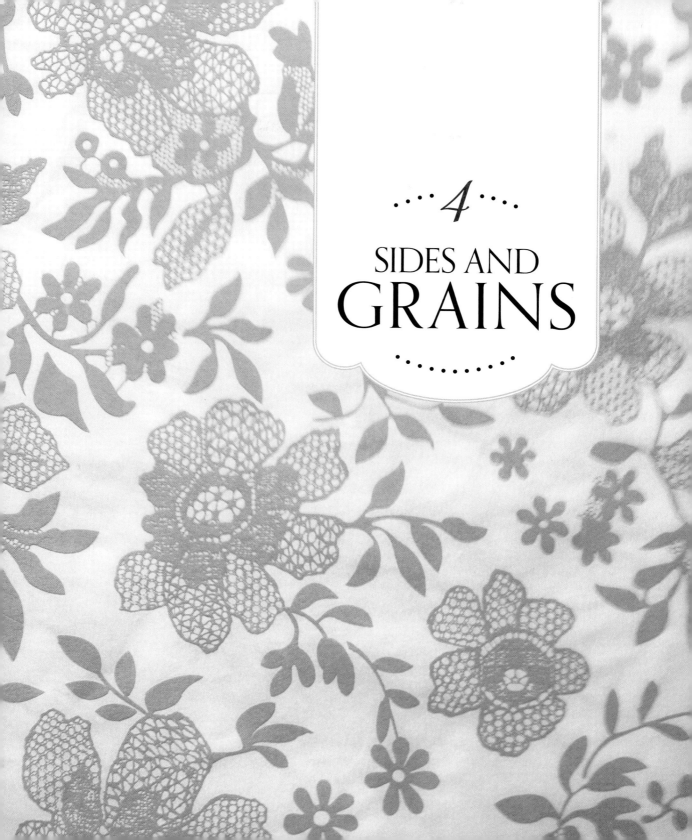

··· *4* ···

# SIDES AND
# GRAINS

TINY GREEN PLANTS are enticingly displayed in the garden center, and before I know it, my shopping cart is filled with the promise of homegrown squash, zucchini, and tomatoes roasting succulently in my oven. Once my dad tills our small garden patch, I delicately place the plants in rows. Then I'm back in my kitchen, happily planning menus and creating recipes for my favorite sides, such as peas and okra.

# Braised Cabbage with Bacon and Onions

It's a Southern tradition to eat black-eyed peas on New Year's Eve to bring you luck and cabbage on New Year's Day to bring you wealth. But once you try this delicious side dish, you won't want to until New Year's Day to enjoy cabbage. To infuse my cabbage with the most flavor, I braise it in chicken broth with bacon and onions.

3 slices bacon

2¼ cups reduced-sodium chicken broth

½ head cabbage, sliced into 4 wedges (keep them intact)

½ yellow onion, thinly sliced

Salt, to taste

¼ teaspoon ground black pepper

Cook the bacon in a large deep skillet until crispy, 6 to 8 minutes. Transfer to a paper towel–lined plate to drain. When cool enough to handle, chop the bacon into small pieces.

Stir ¼ cup of the broth into the bacon fat in the skillet. Bring to a simmer, scraping up the bacon bits in the bottom of the pan. Add the cabbage and onion slices. Season with the salt and pepper. Cook over medium heat for 5 minutes. Add the remaining 2 cups broth, cover, and cook for 8 minutes to reduce the liquid. Reduce the heat to low and cook, covered, until the cabbage is tender, 15 to 20 minutes.

Transfer to a serving bowl and top with bacon pieces. Serve hot.

Serves 4

# Roasted Brussels Sprouts

Brussels sprouts are one of those vegetables that people tend to love or hate. Many people are turned off by their bitterness, but the trick to making delicious sprouts is the cooking method you choose. I find that slowly roasting the sprouts with a little garlic and onion brings out their nutty sweetness and creates the perfect texture—crunchy on the outside and tender on the inside.

30 Brussels sprouts, stem ends trimmed and loose outer leaves discarded

½ onion, sliced

¼ cup plus 2 tablespoons extra-virgin olive oil

2 garlic cloves, minced

1 teaspoon salt

¼ teaspoon ground black pepper

Preheat the oven to 400°F.

Fill a large pot halfway with water and bring to a boil over high heat. Add the Brussels sprouts and cook for 2 minutes to blanch. Remove with a slotted spoon and drain in a sieve. Pat the Brussels sprouts dry with paper towels or a kitchen towel.

Place the Brussels sprouts and onion slices in a rimmed baking sheet. Drizzle the oil over the vegetables and toss to coat. Sprinkle with the garlic, salt, and pepper.

Bake until lightly crispy, 30 to 35 minutes, turning halfway through.

Serves 4

# Creamed Collard Greens

Because collard greens can be slightly bitter, many people shy away from cooking them. My method of preparing collards—blanching the leaves, cutting them into thin strips, and pureeing them with a rich cream sauce—transforms this underrated green into a *MasterChef*-worthy dish.

2 tablespoons unsalted butter

¼ cup diced yellow onion

1 garlic clove, minced

1½ cups heavy cream

½ teaspoon salt

10 large collard green leaves, washed and ribs removed

½ cup reduced-sodium chicken broth

Melt the butter in a large skillet over medium heat. Add the onion and cook until translucent, about 3 minutes. Add the garlic and cook until fragrant, about 1 minute. Stir in 1 cup of the cream and cook for 5 minutes. Reduce the heat to a simmer and cook, stirring occasionally, until the cream has reduced and thickened, about 10 minutes. Stir in the salt.

Bring a pot of salted water to a boil over high heat. Add the collard greens and cook for 2 minutes to blanch. Drain the leaves and pat dry with paper towels. Stack the leaves and roll into a cigar. Cut the cigar in half lengthwise and thinly slice crosswise into long strips.

Add the greens to the cream sauce. Using a hand blender, blend or pulse greens until they are in small pieces. (Or transfer to a countertop blender, puree, and return creamed greens to the pan.) Cook over medium-low heat for 5 minutes, stirring occasionally. Add the chicken broth and remaining ½ cup cream. Stir until combined and cook over medium-low heat until the mixture is heated through, about 10 minutes.

Serves 4

# Carrot Soufflé

Having trouble getting your kids or family members to eat their vegetables? I know how you feel. My sister Brittyn will not eat carrots unless they are in the form of this carrot soufflé, or what I like to call "vegetable candy." This sweet dish is a requested favorite for holidays at our house.

2 teaspoons unsalted butter, at room temperature, plus 6 tablespoons unsalted butter, melted

2½ cups shredded carrots

1 tablespoon plus ¼ cup sugar

1 large egg, separated

1½ tablespoons all-purpose flour

½ teaspoon baking powder

Pinch of ground cinnamon

Boiling water, for the baking dish

Preheat the oven to 350°F. Grease five 10-ounce ramekins with 1 teaspoon of the softened butter. Place the ramekins in a glass baking dish large enough to hold them.

Combine the shredded carrots and water to just barely cover in a medium saucepan. Add 1 tablespoon of the sugar and the remaining 1 teaspoon softened butter. Cook over medium heat until the carrots are soft, 2 to 4 minutes. Drain the carrots and transfer to a food processor. Puree until smooth.

Pour the carrot puree into a medium bowl. Stir in the melted butter and remaining ¼ cup sugar. Stir in the egg yolk. Stir in the flour, baking powder, and cinnamon until combined.

In a separate bowl, using an electric mixer, beat the egg white until soft peaks form. Gently fold the egg white into the carrot mixture. Spoon the carrot mixture into the ramekins.

Pour enough boiling water into the baking dish to come one-quarter of the way up the sides of the ramekins. Bake until the soufflés are set and bubbling, 30 to 35 minutes.

Remove the ramekins from the baking dish with metal tongs and transfer to a wire rack to cool for 5 minutes before serving. Serve in the ramekins.

Serves 5

# Dillicious Potato Salad

In the South we have an ongoing debate raging over the use of sweet or dill pickles in recipes. My potato salad settles the debate by using fresh dill as well as chopped sweet gherkins. The bright, fresh taste of the dill is a nice complement to the pungent, sweet gherkins. No matter which side of the pickle fence you're on, this potato salad is a winner.

4 cups red potatoes, cut into 1-inch cubes

2 hard-boiled eggs, diced

5 tablespoons diced sweet gherkins

1 teaspoon chopped fresh dill

5 tablespoons mayonnaise

¼ teaspoon yellow mustard

1 tablespoon herb mix from the Buttermilk Herb Dressing (page 160)

½ teaspoon mustard powder

¼ teaspoon salt

¼ teaspoon ground black pepper

Combine the potatoes and water to barely cover in a medium saucepan. Bring to boil over high heat. Reduce the heat to a gentle simmer and cook until potatoes are almost fork-tender, 3 to 5 minutes. Drain well and spread the potatoes in an even layer on a kitchen towel. Let them sit for a few minutes so the moisture can evaporate.

Transfer the potatoes to a large bowl. Add the eggs, gherkins, and dill. Stir to combine.

In a separate small bowl, whisk together the mayonnaise, yellow mustard, herb mix, mustard powder, salt, and pepper. Stir the dressing into the potato mixture.

Serves 4 to 6

# Cracked Black Pepper Jasmine Rice-otto

Rice is a versatile grain and inexpensive pantry staple, not to mention a mainstay on many Southern menus. While a traditional risotto is made with Arborio rice and can take an hour or more to prepare, this quick and easy "imposter" version uses fragrant jasmine rice and is ready in less than 30 minutes.

2¼ cups chicken broth

⅔ cup half-and-half

1 tablespoon extra-virgin olive oil

⅓ cup minced yellow onion

1 garlic clove, minced

1 cup jasmine rice*

3 tablespoons dry white wine

⅛ teaspoon fine sea salt

¼ teaspoon cracked black pepper

*Choose a jasmine rice that states on the package that the cooking time is 15 minutes.

Heat the broth in a medium saucepan over medium heat. (Do not boil.) Heat the half-and-half in a small saucepan over medium-low heat until warm.

Meanwhile, heat the oil in a medium saucepan over medium heat. Add the onion and garlic and cook until the onion is translucent, 4 to 5 minutes. Stir in the rice and cook, stirring constantly, until the rice is coated and lightly toasted, about 2 minutes. Add the wine and stir until it has evaporated. Add the salt.

Ladle enough hot broth into the saucepan to barely cover the rice. Bring the broth to a boil over medium-high heat, then reduce the heat to medium. Continue cooking, stirring, and adding small amounts of broth to the rice mixture. Once the broth is done, repeat the process with the warm half-and-half. The rice mixture will become thick and creamy. This whole process should take 22 to 26 minutes. Remove from the heat and stir in the cracked black pepper.

Serve immediately.

Serves 4

# Cauliflower "Mac 'n' Cheese"

Who doesn't love a side of mac 'n' cheese with their fried chicken? My version of this indulgent side dish swaps pasta for cauliflower. Roasting the cauliflower adds a nutty flavor and hearty texture to the dish. You'll never miss the pasta in this "mac 'n' cheese."

8 cups cauliflower florets (about 1 head)

2 tablespoons extra-virgin olive oil

$\frac{1}{2}$ teaspoon kosher salt

$\frac{1}{2}$ teaspoon ground black pepper

2 tablespoons unsalted butter

2 tablespoons all-purpose flour

$1\frac{1}{2}$ cups fat-free milk

$\frac{1}{2}$ cup heavy cream

$\frac{3}{8}$ teaspoon table salt

1 cup grated sharp Cheddar cheese (4 ounces)

Preheat the oven to 400°F.

Toss the cauliflower florets in the oil on a baking sheet. Sprinkle with the kosher salt and $\frac{1}{4}$ teaspoon of the pepper. Roast until fork-tender and lightly browned in spots, 25 to 30 minutes. Remove from the oven but leave the oven on and reduce the temperature to 350°F.

Meanwhile, melt the butter in a medium skillet over medium heat. Stir in the flour and cook for 1 minute. Gradually whisk in the milk. Simmer over medium heat, stirring frequently, until thickened, 2 to 4 minutes. Whisk in the cream and cook for 5 minutes. Reduce the heat to low and stir in all but 2 tablespoons of the cheese, the table salt, and the remaining $\frac{1}{4}$ teaspoon pepper. Stir until the cheese melts, then cook, stirring often, until thickened, 8 to 10 minutes.

Place the cauliflower florets in an 8 x 8-inch glass baking dish or four 10-ounce ramekins. Pour the cheese sauce on top. Sprinkle the top of the cauliflower with the remaining 2 tablespoons cheese.

Bake until the cheese is bubbling, 20 to 25 minutes. Serve warm.

Serves 4

# Creole Succotash

During the Great Depression, succotash was a staple eaten in many homes—it was cheap to make and composed of nutritious and abundant vegetables. These same features make succotash a popular dish today. My "Creole" version incorporates okra and tomatoes in addition to the traditional lima beans and corn. I like to serve it alongside fish and chicken dishes such as Oven-Fried Catfish (page 89) and Butter- and Herb-Roasted Chicken (page 97).

½ cup fresh okra slices (½ inch thick)

2 teaspoons unsalted butter

1 tablespoon extra-virgin olive oil

1 cup fresh or frozen lima beans

1 ear corn, kernels cut off (about ½ cup)

¼ cup diced yellow onion

¼ teaspoon minced garlic

⅛ teaspoon cracked black pepper

15 grape tomatoes, halved

Salt and ground black pepper

Bring a small pot of water to a boil. Boil the okra slices for 1 minute. Drain and rinse the slime off the okra. Bring more water to a boil in the pot and repeat the boiling and rinsing process. Set aside.

Melt the butter in the oil in a large skillet over medium heat. Add the lima beans, corn, onion, garlic, okra, and cracked pepper to the pan and cook, stirring occasionally, until the onion is translucent and the beans are tender, about 5 minutes.

Add the tomatoes and cook for 1 minute to heat through. Season to taste with salt and pepper. Serve warm.

Serves 4

# Creamy Mashed Potatoes with White Andouille Gravy

Making perfect mashed potatoes is an art form. For me, perfect mashed potatoes must be creamy (no lumps!) and have real potato flavor. I use a food mill to produce a smooth, even texture and add butter and cream to enhance the natural flavor of the potatoes. Served with a side of White Andouille Gravy, these fluffy potatoes are truly heavenly.

**MASHED POTATOES**

3 large baking potatoes

Salt

1 teaspoon unsalted butter

8 tablespoons (1 stick) unsalted butter, melted

1 cup heavy cream

Ground black pepper

**WHITE ANDOUILLE GRAVY**

7 ounces fresh andouille sausage, casings removed

2 tablespoons all-purpose flour

1¼ cups fat-free milk

Salt and ground black pepper

To make the mashed potatoes: Peel the potatoes and cut into 1-inch cubes. Combine the potatoes and water to cover by 1 inch in a large saucepan. Add ½ teaspoon salt and the 1 teaspoon butter to the water. Bring to a boil, then immediately reduce to a gentle simmer and cook until the potato cubes are fork-tender, 20 to 25 minutes.

While the potatoes are cooking, heat the cream in a heavy-bottomed saucepan over medium-low heat until warmed through but not boiling, about 4 minutes.

Drain the potatoes. Use a food mill or ricer to cream the potatoes into a bowl. Stir in the melted butter. Then stir in ¾ cup of the warmed cream. Add more cream if desired for a thinner consistency. Season with salt and pepper to taste.

To make the gravy: Heat a medium cast-iron skillet over medium-high heat. Add the sausage and break it up into small pieces with a wooden spoon. Cook until browned and cooked through, about 8 minutes. Remove the sausage with a slotted spoon and transfer to a paper towel–lined plate to drain.

Whisk the flour into the fat in the skillet and cook over medium heat for 1 minute. Whisking constantly, add ½ cup of the milk. Gradually add the remaining ¾ cup milk and cook, stirring often, until the gravy has thickened, about 6 minutes. Season with salt and pepper to taste. Add the cooked sausage to the gravy and cook for 1 minute to heat through.

Transfer the potatoes to a serving bowl and serve hot with the gravy.

Serves 4 to 6

# Field Peas with Okra and Andouille Sausage

Field peas have a soft, creamy texture. One of the signs of summer for me is a big pot of field peas and okra simmering on the stove top. In the South, these are usually served with squares of crunchy cornbread and slices of fresh juicy tomatoes. I like to make my peas and okra with andouille sausage and serve over rice for a hearty, filling meal.

1 teaspoon extra-virgin olive oil

¼ pound andouille sausage links, cut into 1-inch pieces

3 cups fresh or frozen field peas (lady peas or black-eyed peas may be substituted)

10 fresh whole okra pods

6 fresh basil leaves, torn into pieces

Salt and ground black pepper

Heat the oil in a medium saucepan over medium heat. Add the andouille and cook, stirring occasionally, until the sausage begins to render its fat, 2 to 4 minutes.

Add the field peas, okra, and enough water to cover by 1 inch. Bring to a boil, reduce to a simmer, cover, and cook until the peas and okra are tender, 40 to 45 minutes.

Stir in the basil. Season to taste with salt and pepper.

Serves 4 to 6

# Sweet and Spicy Coleslaw

Making coleslaw from scratch has long been a tradition in my extended family. My mom remembers her Grandma McCarter making coleslaw using ingredients fresh from her garden. My recipe is a different take on the old Southern favorite. The sweetness and heat in this coleslaw pairs nicely with almost any seafood dish. I love serving it with my crab cakes (page 33).

**CABBAGE**

½ head red cabbage, halved, cored, and sliced thinly

¼ red onion, thinly sliced

**SWEET JALAPEÑO AND PECAN VINAIGRETTE**

¼ cup pecan halves, toasted

¼ cup sugar

1 tablespoon finely chopped fresh jalapeño pepper

3 tablespoons apple cider vinegar

2 tablespoons balsamic vinegar

¾ teaspoon fresh lemon juice

⅛ teaspoon celery seed

⅛ teaspoon salt

⅛ teaspoon ground black pepper

3 tablespoons extra-virgin olive oil

To prepare the cabbage: Combine the cabbage and onion in a large bowl.

Combine the pecan halves, sugar, pepper, the vinegars, lemon juice, celery seed, salt, and pepper in a blender. Blend to combine. Remove the cap from the center of the blender's lid. With the blender on low, drizzle in the oil until combined.

Toss the cabbage mixture with the vinaigrette. Chill in the refrigerator for at least 30 minutes. Before serving, adjust the seasoning with more salt and pepper to taste.

Serves 4

# Grandmother Adele's Dressing with a Twist

The original version of this recipe was created by my Grandmother Adele. She typically served her dressing at holidays like Thanksgiving and Christmas, as part of a turkey dinner. While I've kept her delicious recipe largely intact, I've added fresh herbs to brighten up the flavor and created individual portion sizes, making it easy to serve for any occasion.

2½ cups crumbled cornbread

1 cup torn white bread

½ medium onion, quartered

½ cup thickly sliced celery

1 large egg, well beaten

1 hard-boiled egg, finely diced

1 teaspoon fresh thyme leaves

1½ teaspoons minced fresh sage

½ teaspoon minced fresh rosemary

½ teaspoon salt

¼ teaspoon ground black pepper

2 cups chicken broth

4 tablespoons (½ stick) unsalted butter, melted

Preheat the oven to 350°F. Coat 6 small quiche or tart pans (about 4½ inches wide and 1 inch tall or holding about ½ cup each) with cooking spray.

Combine the cornbread and white bread in a medium bowl. Combine the onion and celery in a food processor and pulse until fine. Add to the bread mixture and stir to combine.

Add the beaten egg, hard-boiled egg, herbs, salt, and pepper and mix together well. Add the broth and melted butter. Stir to combine.

Divide the dressing mixture among the prepared pans. Place the pans on a baking sheet and bake until lightly browned around the edges and the middle is set, 30 to 35 minutes. Transfer to a rack to cool for 5 minutes. Carefully remove the dressings from the pans and place on individual plates to serve.

Serves 6

# Turnip Greens Pesto Pasta Salad

Driving through the South in the fall, you'll see gardens overflowing with greens. Turnip greens are an often-overlooked ingredient and they are full of nutrients and delicious when cooked. I use this versatile "pesto" with my Rosemary Focaccia for an appetizer (see the opposite page) as well as in this simple pasta salad that can be served hot or cold.

3 cups small pasta shapes (bow-ties or penne work well)

Turnip Green Pesto (page 164)

5 oil-packed sun-dried tomatoes, thinly sliced

1 tablespoon grated Parmesan cheese

Bring a large pot of water to a boil. Season with salt. Stir in the pasta and cook according to the package directions.

Drain the pasta and transfer to a large bowl. While the pasta is still warm, add the pesto and toss to coat. Add the sun-dried tomatoes and toss to combine.

If serving warm, top with Parmesan cheese immediately. If serving cold, refrigerate for 1 to 2 hours and sprinkle with the cheese just before serving.

Serves 4

A curtain panel or yard of fabric can make an inexpensive and elegant runner or tablecloth to use when decorating for a special occasion. Look for fabric that goes with your theme and enhances your table setting.

# Rosemary Focaccia

Homemade bread adds a special touch to any dish, from everyday sandwiches to elegant entrées. My Nanny Ida always had a loaf of homemade bread on the table when I came to visit, and she taught me that making bread doesn't have to be a daunting task. This recipe is so quick and easy to prepare that soon you'll always have fresh bread on hand, too! The dough can also be used to make a delicious pizza crust.

1 envelope ($\frac{1}{4}$ ounce) active dry yeast

1$\frac{2}{3}$ cups lukewarm (100° to 110°F) water

4 cups plus 3 tablespoons bread flour

$\frac{1}{4}$ cup plus 3 tablespoons extra-virgin olive oil, plus extra for greasing the pan

2$\frac{1}{2}$ teaspoons salt

1 teaspoon plus 1 tablespoon chopped fresh rosemary

1 teaspoon kosher salt

Combine the yeast and water in the bowl of a stand mixer. Let stand for 5 minutes until dissolved.

Add 4 cups of the flour, $\frac{1}{4}$ cup of the oil, and the salt to the mixer bowl. Using the paddle attachment, beat on medium speed until the dough is smooth. Add 1 teaspoon of the rosemary. Replace the paddle with the dough hook and increase the speed to high. After about 4 minutes, the dough should form and be sticky.

Sprinkle the remaining 3 tablespoons flour on a work surface. Turn the dough out onto the surface and knead in the flour. Form the dough into a smooth ball. Place the dough into a lightly oiled bowl and turn the dough to coat. Cover the bowl with plastic wrap and let rise until doubled in size, about 1 hour.

Coat a 13 x 9-inch baking pan with oil. Press the dough into the pan. Cover the dough with a kitchen towel and let rise for 1 hour.

Meanwhile, preheat the oven to 475°F.

Drizzle the remaining 3 tablespoons oil over the bread and make shallow indentations into the dough in rows. Sprinkle the remaining 1 tablespoons rosemary and the salt over the dough. Bake until the top is lightly browned, 12 to 14 minutes.

Remove the bread from the pan to a rack to cool before slicing.

Serves 6 to 8

# Jalapeño Cornbread

The secret to creating a crunchy outer crust for your cornbread is using a hot cast-iron skillet. This technique was passed down to me from my mom who learned from her mom and grandmother. I like to spice up my cornbread with diced jalapeños. Feel free to add more or less than called for below, depending on how much heat you prefer. I cut my cornbread into triangle wedges and serve it warm with butter.

2 cups fine ground cornmeal

1 tablespoon baking powder

1 teaspoon salt

1 large egg

$\frac{1}{2}$ cup low-fat buttermilk

$\frac{3}{4}$ cup fat-free milk

$\frac{1}{4}$ cup plus 1$\frac{1}{2}$ tablespoons canola oil

$\frac{1}{2}$ cup corn kernels

3 tablespoons shredded Cheddar cheese

2 tablespoon diced fresh jalapeño peppers

Preheat the oven to 450°F.

Mix the cornmeal, baking powder, and salt in a large bowl. Add the egg, buttermilk, fat-free milk, and $\frac{1}{4}$ cup of the oil and stir until well combined. Mix in the corn, cheese, and jalapeños.

Add the remaining 1$\frac{1}{2}$ tablespoons oil to 9-inch cast-iron skillet. Rub the oil around to thoroughly coat the bottom and sides of the skillet. Heat in the oven for 6 minutes. Remove from the oven and pour in the batter.

Bake until the crust is golden, 25 to 30 minutes. Cut into wedges and serve hot.

Serves 4 to 6

# 5

## ELEGANT
# ENTRÉES

I KICK OFF MY FLIP-FLOPS, put on my heels, and pick up my stemmed glass of "Southern wine," aka sweet tea. Decorative touches make an everyday meal special, and my friends and family deserve the best. In the *MasterChef* kitchen, I had an assortment of dishware to choose from when plating for the judges. At home, my culinary creations are elegantly displayed on vintage and unusual dishware, results from my explorations of flea markets and garage sales. Presentation counts!

# Shrimp Bisque and Grits

Even in the South, most people are nervous about eating "grits" for any meal other than breakfast. But once they taste my cheesy Parmesan grits, they quickly change their minds! I top my grits with a creamy, spicy shrimp bisque. Try serving it with slices of crusty French bread or Jalapeño Cornbread (page 83) so your guests can sop up the extra sauce.

## SHRIMP BISQUE

4 tablespoons (½ stick) unsalted butter

¼ cup diced yellow onion

2 garlic cloves, minced

5 tablespoons all-purpose flour

3 cups reduced-sodium chicken broth

2 cups heavy cream

1 cup corn kernels

1½ cups fresh or drained canned diced tomatoes

3 links (½ pound) andouille sausage, halved lengthwise, cut crosswise into ½-inch slices

1 pound medium shrimp, peeled, deveined

2 teaspoons crab boil seasoning

¼ teaspoon salt

⅛ teaspoon ground black pepper

## PARMESAN GRITS

¾ teaspoon salt

1½ cups quick-cooking grits

4 tablespoons (½ stick) unsalted butter

1 cup freshly grated Parmesan cheese (4 ounces)

2 tablespoons heavy cream

⅛ teaspoon ground black pepper

## GARNISH

¼ cup chopped scallions

To make the shrimp bisque: Melt the butter in a large saucepan over medium heat. Add the onion and cook until translucent, 3 to 4 minutes. Add the garlic and cook until fragrant, about 2 minutes. Stir in the flour and cook for 1 minute. Whisking constantly, gradually add the broth. Stir in the cream. Add the corn and canned diced tomatoes (if using fresh, don't add them until the end or they'll fall apart). Cook over medium heat for 15 minutes to melt the flavors.

Meanwhile, cook the sausage in a medium skillet over medium-high heat. Cook until heated through and lightly browned, about 8 minutes. Drain on a paper towel–lined plate.

Add the sausage to the bisque. Reduce the heat to low and cook for 5 minutes.

Toss the shrimp and crab boil seasoning together in a small bowl. Add to the bisque. Cook until the shrimp are opaque throughout, about 8 minutes. Remove from the heat, cover, and set aside.

To make the parmesan grits: Bring 5 cups water to a boil in a medium saucepan over high heat. Add ¼ teaspoon of the salt. Stir in the grits. Reduce the heat to low and cook for 5 minutes. Stir in the butter, Parmesan, cream, pepper, and remaining ½ teaspoon salt. Cook for 5 minutes to melt the cheese.

To serve, spoon the grits into shallow bowls. Top with shrimp bisque. Garnish with scallions.

Serves 4 to 6

# Oven-Fried Catfish with Fresh Dill Tartar Sauce

Eating out on Thursday, Friday, or Saturday night in the South usually includes dining at a catfish house. A typical catfish house features a menu of fried whole catfish or fillets, coleslaw, fries, and hushpuppies. My cookbook would not be complete without a recipe for my variation on this tradition: baked catfish served with fresh dill tartar sauce.

## CATFISH

1 cup low-fat buttermilk

4 catfish fillets (about 1/2 pound each)

3/4 cup fine-grind cornmeal

3/4 teaspoon onion powder

1/4 teaspoon garlic powder

1/2 teaspoon lemon-pepper seasoning

1/2 teaspoon salt

1/4 teaspoon crushed freeze-dried chives

Pinch of cayenne pepper

2 tablespoons canola oil

## TARTAR SAUCE

1 cup mayonnaise

2 teaspoons stone-ground mustard

1 teaspoon grated lemon zest

1 teaspoon fresh lemon juice

1/2 teaspoon ground black pepper

3/4 teaspoon minced fresh dill

3/4 teaspoon minced fresh chives

To prepare the fish: Pour the buttermilk into a shallow baking dish. Place the catfish fillets in the buttermilk and turn to coat. Refrigerate for 25 minutes.

Preheat the oven to 400°F.

Combine the cornmeal, onion powder, garlic powder, lemon-pepper seasoning, salt, chives, and cayenne in a shallow dish or pie plate.

Pour the oil into a large cast-iron skillet and turn to coat the bottom. Place in the oven to heat for 6 minutes.

Working with 1 fillet at a time, shake off the excess buttermilk and dredge in the cornmeal mixture to coat.

Place cornmeal-coated fillets in the preheated skillet. Bake for 10 minutes. Turn the fillets and bake until golden brown and crisp, 10 to 15 minutes (depending on the size of the fillets).

Meanwhile, to make the tartar sauce: Mix all the ingredients together in a small bowl.

Serve the hot fish with the tartar sauce.

Serves 4

# Shrimp and Sausage with Grits Soufflé and Yellow Pepper Sabayon

This is my upscale version of shrimp and grits. It's made with pan-seared shrimp, andouille sausage, and roasted corn fresh off the cob. The grits soufflé is surrounded by a yellow pepper sabayon, which is the French name for a thick, creamy sauce. This dish takes a little time to prepare, but it is absolutely mouth-watering and definitely worth the effort.

### CORN

3 ears corn, unhusked

3 tablespoons unsalted butter

$\frac{1}{2}$ teaspoon salt

$\frac{1}{2}$ teaspoon ground black pepper

### SABAYON

2 tablespoons extra-virgin olive oil

$\frac{1}{2}$ cup diced yellow onion

$\frac{1}{4}$ cup diced yellow bell pepper

1 garlic clove, minced

$1\frac{1}{2}$ cups heavy cream

1 teaspoon salt

1 large egg yolk

### GRITS SOUFFLÉ

2 cups whole milk

$\frac{1}{2}$ cup quick-cooking grits

$\frac{1}{2}$ teaspoon salt

$\frac{1}{8}$ teaspoon ground black pepper

2 tablespoons unsalted butter

$\frac{1}{2}$ cup shredded sharp Cheddar cheese (2 ounces)

2 eggs, separated

Preheat the oven to 400°F. Grease six 8- to 10-ounce soufflé dishes and refrigerate.

To prepare the corn: Peel the husk back, remove the silk, and rub each cob with 1 tablespoon butter and sprinkle with the salt and pepper. Replace the husk and place on a baking sheet. Bake until lightly browned, about 20 minutes. (Leave the oven on but reduce the temperature to 375°F for the soufflés.) When the corn is cool enough to handle, pull back the husks and slice the kernels off the cobs into a bowl. Set aside for using in the sabayon and as a garnish.

Meanwhile, to make the sabayon: Heat the oil in a medium skillet over medium heat. Add the onion and bell pepper and cook until softened, about 5 minutes. Add the garlic and cook until fragrant, about 2 minutes. Add the cream and 1 cup of the corn and cook over medium heat until the cream thickens and the corn is heated through, about 4 minutes. Transfer the mixture to a blender and puree. Set aside while you start the soufflés.

To prepare the grits soufflés: Bring the milk to a slight boil in a medium saucepan over medium-high heat. Stir in the grits and cook, stirring occasionally, until the grits reach a porridge consistency, about 5 minutes. Remove from the heat and let cool slightly. Stir in the salt, pepper, butter, Cheddar, and egg yolks.

With an electric mixer, beat the egg whites until stiff peaks form. Fold the egg whites into the grits mixture. Remove the soufflé dishes from the refrigerator and fill with the grits mixture. Place the dishes on a baking sheet and bake until the soufflés are just set, 18 to 20 minutes.

*(continued on page 92)*

1 pound large shrimp, peeled and deveined

¼ teaspoon salt

¼ teaspoon ground black pepper

Dash of cayenne pepper

2 tablespoons extra-virgin olive oil

8 ounces andouille sausage, cut on the diagonal into 1-inch slices

GARNISH

¼ cup chopped scallions

1 tablespoon chopped fresh parsley

While the soufflés are baking, finish the sabayon. Place a sieve over the top of a double boiler and strain the pureed sabayon mixture through it. Bring water to a simmer in the bottom of the double boiler. Place the strained cream mixture over the simmering water. Sprinkle in the salt. Whisk in the egg yolk and continue whisking over the simmer water until the sauce thickens, 5 to 8 minutes. The sauce should coat the back of a spoon. Remove from the heat and cover to keep warm while you cook the shrimp and sausage.

To make the shrimp and sausage: Toss the shrimp with salt, black pepper, and cayenne in a bowl. Heat the oil in a medium skillet over medium-high heat. Add the shrimp and cook for 2 minutes on the first side, and 1 minute on the second side or until pink and opaque through. Transfer the shrimp to a plate.

In the same skillet, cook the sausage until browned and cooked through, about 5 minutes. Remove from pan and drain on a paper towel–lined plate. Cover to keep warm.

When the soufflés are done, assemble the plates: Spoon the sabayon sauce in the middle of a plate. Unmold a soufflé onto the sauce. Top with some sausage, shrimp, and some of the remaining corn. Sprinkle with the scallions and parsley.

Serves 6

# Cranberry Chipotle BBQ Chicken with Potato Salad

Whether you're entertaining indoors for game day or tailgating outdoors, BBQ is always a favorite. My dad, "Coach Miller," is the host of our high school's tailgating cookout. He always wants to impress the guys with great food and that is when I come in to help. What makes this BBQ chicken stand out is the unique flavor of the cranberry chipotle BBQ sauce. The contrast of the sweet to the heat creates a great surprise for the palate. This BBQ chicken is a winner at our tailgate and I know it will be for you, too!

### CRANBERRY CHIPOTLE BBQ SAUCE

1 tablespoon vegetable oil

½ cup diced yellow onion

2 cloves garlic, minced

¼ teaspoon soy sauce

¼ teaspoon Worchestershire sauce

1 cup dark brown sugar

1 cup tomato puree

¼ teaspoon molasses

1 cup jellied cranberry sauce

2 chipotle peppers in adobo

1 tablespoon adobo sauce

½ teaspoon salt

1 tablespoon apple cider vinegar

### CHICKEN BREAST

4 bone-in split chicken breasts

Salt and pepper

2 teaspoons peanut oil

To make the BBQ sauce: Heat the vegtetable oil in a small saucepan over medium heat. Add the onion and cook, stirring occasionally, until translucent, 4 to 6 minutes. Add the garlic and cook 1 minute more. Add the soy sauce, Worchestershire sauce, brown sugar, tomato puree, molasses, cranberry sauce, peppers, adobo sauce, salt, and vinegar and bring to a boil. Reduce to a gentle simmer and cook, stirring often, 45 minutes or until the sauce has thickened. Remove the sauce to a bowl and let cool.

To make the chicken: Preheat the oven to 350°F. Generously season the chicken breasts all over with salt and pepper. Heat a heavy oven-safe skillet over medium-high heat, and add the peanut oil. Sear the breasts, skin-side down, until brown, 2 to 4 minutes. Turn the breasts skin-side up and brush with just enough of the BBQ sauce to coat them. Put the pan in the oven and cook the breasts 35 to 45 minutes, or until a meat thermometer inserted into the thickest part of the breast reaches 160°F. Remove the chicken breasts from the pan and let rest for 10 minutes. Serve with Potato Salad (page 95) and grilled asparagus, if you like.

Serves 4

*(continued on page 95)*

# Potato Salad

5 cups sliced tri-color fingerling
   potatoes

$\frac{3}{4}$ cup mayonnaise

2 teaspoons apple cider vinegar

1 tablespoon stone ground mustard

2 teaspoons chopped fresh dill

2 teaspoons chopped fresh parsley

1 finely grated boiled egg

$\frac{1}{4}$ teaspoon lemon zest

$\frac{1}{4}$ teaspoon cayenne

$\frac{1}{4}$ teaspoon celery seed

1 tablespoon chopped pickled
   jalapeños

$\frac{1}{2}$ teaspoon jalapeño juice

$\frac{1}{3}$ cup diced celery

$\frac{1}{3}$ cup diced sweet onion

Salt and pepper to taste

Slice the fingerlings into $\frac{1}{4}$-inch-thick slices and put them into a medium saucepan. Add enough cold water to barely cover them. Bring to a boil. Reduce to a gentle simmer so the potatoes do not break up when cooking. Cook them for 5 to 7 minutes, or until the tip of a sharp knife slightly resists when inserted into one of the slices. Drain the potatoes in a colander, then spread them out on a kitchen towel to dry just until barely cool, about 5 minutes.

In a medium bowl, mix together the mayonnaise, vinegar, mustard, dill, parsley, egg, lemon zest, cayenne, celery seed, jalapeños, and juice.

Put the potatoes into a large bowl, and add the celery and sweet onion. Toss with a little of the dressing at a time until coated. Season to taste with salt and pepper.

Serves 4

# Butter- and Herb-Roasted Chicken

You don't have to wait for a special occasion or holiday to roast a whole chicken. Growing up, I often went to my great-grandmother's house for big Sunday dinners. A typical Sunday dinner might feature chicken with a homemade cornbread dressing and dumplings. My roasted chicken with fresh herb butter combines traditional comfort food with modern flavor. Served with gravy and dressing, it's a meal that's sure to please your family and impress your guests.

**HERB BUTTER**

2 tablespoons unsalted butter, at room temperature

1 garlic clove, minced

$\frac{1}{2}$ teaspoon chopped fresh sage

$\frac{1}{4}$ teaspoon chopped fresh rosemary

$\frac{1}{8}$ teaspoon fresh thyme leaves

$\frac{1}{2}$ teaspoon kosher salt

$\frac{1}{8}$ teaspoon ground black pepper

**CHICKEN AND GRAVY**

3 celery stalks

3 carrots, halved lengthwise

1 medium yellow onion, sliced

3 garlic cloves, peeled and smashed with the side of a knife

1 chicken (4 to 6 pounds), cut into 8 pieces

Salt and ground black pepper

1 cup chicken broth

2 tablespoons all-purpose flour

Grandmother Adele's Dressing with a Twist (page 79)

Preheat the oven to 400°F.

To make the herb butter: Mix all the ingredients together.

To prepare the chicken: Place the celery, carrots, onion slices, and garlic cloves in the bottom of a roasting pan or large glass baking dish. Lay the chicken pieces on top of the vegetables. Season the chicken all over with $\frac{1}{2}$ teaspoon salt and $\frac{1}{4}$ teaspoon pepper.

Rub the herb butter under the skin and on top of each piece of chicken.

Pour the broth into the bottom of the roasting pan. Bake the chicken until a thermometer inserted in the thickest part of the thigh registers 165°F, about 1 hour. Transfer the roasted chicken to a serving platter. Strain the cooking juices from the roasting pan into a bowl. Discard the vegetables.

To make the pan gravy: Pour 1 cup of the strained cooking juices into a medium saucepan. Bring to a simmer over medium heat. Whisk in the flour. Cook until the gravy has thickened, 3 to 4 minutes. Stir in a little water if the gravy becomes too thick. Season the gravy with salt and pepper to taste.

To serve, spoon pan gravy onto each plate and top with the dressing and roasted chicken.

Serves 4

# Buttermilk Pan-Fried Chicken

Under the pressure of the clock in the *MasterChef* Season 1 finale, I dropped my buttermilk pan-fried chicken on the floor! I knew I had to press on; I battered and pan-fried another piece of chicken. With the Lord watching over me, I cooked it in an amazing 7 minutes. When asked how I did it, I replied, "The secret ingredient was prayer!" In this quick, easy recipe the chicken is pan-fried on the stovetop and finished in the oven for even browning and cooking.

3 boneless, skinless chicken breast halves (about 6 ounces each)

1 teaspoon salt

1/4 teaspoon ground black pepper

1 cup buttermilk

1 large egg

Pinch of cayenne pepper

1 cup all-purpose flour

3 tablespoons canola oil

Preheat the oven to 400°F. Coat a baking sheet with cooking spray.

Season both sides of the chicken with 1/2 teaspoon of the salt and 1/8 teaspoon of the black pepper.

Stir together the buttermilk and egg in a shallow dish. Combine the flour with the cayenne and the remaining 1/2 teaspoon salt and 1/8 teaspoon black pepper on a plate.

Heat the oil in a large skillet over medium-high heat. Dip the chicken in the buttermilk mixture and then coat in the seasoned flour. Carefully place the chicken in the hot oil. Cook for 2 minutes on each side. Remove from the pan and place on the baking sheet. Bake until cooked through but still juicy (about 155°F on an instant-read thermometer), 6 to 8 minutes, depending on the thickness of the chicken.

Drain on a paper towel–lined plate.

Serves 3

# Inside-Out Chicken Pot Pies

These pretty, petite pot pies are served in individual puff pastry cups that have been baked in a muffin tin. The result is an open-faced pot pie rich with vegetables, lemon-pepper chicken, and a homemade Parmesan cream sauce. Hearty and satisfying, these little pies are sure to warm up your guests on a crisp fall evening.

3 boneless, skinless chicken breasts (about 6 ounces each)

1½ tablespoons fresh lemon juice

1 tablespoon lemon-pepper seasoning

5 cups cubed (½ inch) red potatoes

3 cups carrot pieces (carrots quartered lengthwise and cut crosswise into ½-inch pieces)

6 tablespoons unsalted butter

½ cup celery, finely diced

½ yellow onion, diced

2 garlic cloves, minced

1 teaspoon chopped fresh thyme leaves

½ cup all-purpose flour

4 cups reduced-sodium chicken stock

2 cups heavy cream

1 cup fresh corn kernels (from 1 ear)

1 bag (16 ounces) frozen green peas, thawed

2 cups freshly grated Parmesan cheese (about 8 ounces)

1 teaspoon salt

¼ teaspoon ground black pepper

1 teaspoon grated lemon zest

1 box frozen puff pastry, thawed

Preheat the oven to 350°F.

Place the chicken in an 8 × 8-inch glass baking dish. Pour the lemon juice over the chicken. Sprinkle with the lemon-pepper. Add 1 tablespoon water. Cover tightly with foil and bake until chicken is cooked through but still juicy (an instant-read thermometer registers 155°F in the thickest part), 45 to 50 minutes. Transfer to a plate. When cool enough to handle, use 2 forks to shred the chicken.

Combine the potatoes, carrots, and water to cover in a medium saucepan. Bring to a boil. Reduce the heat to medium and cook until the potatoes are fork-tender, about 12 minutes. Drain and set aside.

Melt the butter in a large saucepan over medium-low heat. Add the celery and onion and cook until vegetables are softened, about 5 minutes. Add the garlic and thyme and cook for another minute. Stir in the flour and cook for 1 minute. Gradually whisk in the stock and heavy cream. Add the potatoes, carrots, corn, and peas. Gently simmer over medium heat for 10 minutes to meld the flavors and reduce the liquid; stir often to prevent the cream from sticking. Stir in the Parmesan, salt, pepper, and shredded chicken. Cook for 25 to 30 minutes on low heat, stirring occasionally. Stir in the lemon zest, cover, and remove from heat.

Preheat the oven to 400°F. Cut each sheet of puff pastry into 4 squares. Turn a muffin tin upside down and coat the cups with cooking spray. Place the puff pastry squares over the prepared muffin cups. Poke about 10 holes in the puff pastry with the tip of a knife. Bake until pastry is crisp and golden brown, about 13 minutes. Remove the puff pastry from the muffin tin and let cool slightly on a rack.

Place each puff pastry bowl on a plate. Divide the creamy Parmesan chicken and vegetable mixture among the bowls. Serve immediately.

*Serves 8*

# Bacon-Wrapped Pork Tenderloin with Rosemary-Cranberry Glaze

Cooking a whole pork tenderloin is an easy and inexpensive way to create an elegant meal. Wrapping the tenderloin in bacon not only imparts a rich, smoky flavor to the pork, but also keeps this lean cut of meat moist as it roasts in the oven. Pork pairs well with sweet fruit components. My rosemary-cranberry glaze not only adds sweetness but also an aromatic herbal component.

**GLAZE**

12 ounces fresh cranberries

1²⁄₃ cups sugar

1 sprig rosemary

**PORK**

1 pound pork tenderloin, trimmed of fat and silver skin

¹⁄₂ teaspoon salt

¹⁄₈ teaspoon ground black pepper

17 slices bacon (about ³⁄₄ pound)

To make the glaze: Combine the cranberries and sugar with 1¹⁄₄ cups water in a medium saucepan. Bring to a boil over high heat. Reduce the heat to medium and cook for 15 minutes. Transfer the mixture to a blender and puree. Strain the mixture through a fine-mesh sieve back into the pan, pressing on the solids (discard the cranberry skins and seeds). Add the rosemary to the sauce. Cook for 10 minutes on low heat to infuse with rosemary flavor.

To prepare the pork: Preheat the oven to 400°F. Coat a baking sheet with cooking spray.

Season the pork all over with the salt and pepper. Lay the bacon strips, slightly overlapping each other, on the baking sheet. Lay the pork tenderloin down the center of the bacon strips, perpendicular to them. Carefully wrap the bacon slices on one side of the pork around the tenderloin, tucking the bacon ends under the tenderloin to secure. Roll the tenderloin forward to finish the wrapping of the bacon. Secure bacon ends with toothpicks if loose.

Bake the tenderloin for 25 minutes. Remove from the oven and brush a thick coating of glaze over the tenderloin. Bake until the glaze sets on the pork, 5 to 7 minutes longer. Let the pork rest for 10 minutes before slicing.

Serve the pork slices with any remaining rosemary-cranberry glaze.

Serves 4

# Root Beer-Glazed Ham

Root beer is delicious on its own in a frosty cold mug or paired with scoops of vanilla ice cream in a float, but here I use it as a glaze in a savory, main-dish recipe. The dark rich flavor of the root beer paired with the tartness of apple, sweetness of brown sugar, and aromatic spices makes this ham a show-stopper! I like to serve it with a side of Cauliflower "Mac 'n' Cheese" (page 73). You can get creative and use leftover ham in your Stuffed Muffuletta Po' Boys (page 58).

2 teaspoons cornstarch

2 cans (12 ounces each) root beer

1 Golden Delicious apple, peeled and thinly sliced

¼ cup packed light brown sugar

1 cinnamon stick

4 whole cloves

2 allspice berries

10- to 11-pound bone-in half ham

Whisk 2 teaspoons of water into the cornstarch in a small bowl. Transfer to a small saucepan along with the root beer, apple, brown sugar, cinnamon, cloves, and allspice. Bring to a boil over medium-high heat and cook for 4 minutes to dissolve the sugar. Reduce to a simmer and cook until reduced to about 1 cup, 45 minutes to 1 hour.

Carefully remove and reserve the apples slices (discard the spices). Increase the heat to medium-high and bring the mixture to a boil, whisking constantly. Cook until the mixture has thickened to a slight syrup consistency, about 1 minute. Pour the glaze into a small bowl to cool slightly. The glaze can be made a day ahead of time and refrigerated until ready to use.

Preheat the oven to 400°F.

Place the ham in a deep roasting pan. Using a sharp knife, cut through the top layer of fat and into the meat in a pattern of 1-inch diamonds. Brush half of glaze onto the top of the ham. Pour ½ cup water into the pan. Cover with foil and bake for 1 hour.

Reduce the oven temperature to 250°F and bake for 7 hours, checking periodically to remove pork drippings, as needed. Remove the ham from the oven. Brush the rest of the glaze on the ham. Place the reserved apple slices on top of the glaze. Return to the oven and bake uncovered for 30 minutes.

Allow to rest for at least 30 minutes before slicing. Remove the visible fat if desired and thinly slice the ham. Serve warm.

Serves 8 to 10

# Mini Meat Loaves

Meat loaf is a classic comfort food. When I was growing up, my mother used to make meat loaf for family dinners, and today I love making these mini-loaves when I entertain. The Sun-Dried Tomato and Cranberry Ketchup adds a punch of bright flavor and color to the dish. I like to serve these mini-loaves with Cauliflower "Mac 'n' Cheese" (page 73) or Creamy Mashed Potatoes (page 75).

$\frac{1}{2}$ cup reduced-sodium beef broth

Miracle Marinade (page 159)

$\frac{1}{2}$ pound ground chuck

1$\frac{1}{2}$ pounds lean ground beef

3 tablespoons Italian-style breadcrumbs

2 tablespoons whole milk

1 large egg

1 large egg white

$\frac{1}{8}$ teaspoon coarsely ground black pepper

1 cup Sun-Dried Tomato and Cranberry Ketchup (page 161)

Combine the broth and $\frac{1}{4}$ cup of the Miracle Marinade in a small saucepan. Cook over medium heat until reduced to $\frac{1}{4}$ cup, about 10 minutes.

Preheat the oven to 350°F.

Combine the ground chuck and lean beef in a large bowl. Sprinkle the breadcrumbs over the meat mixture. Pour the milk and reduced marinade mixture over the breadcrumbs to moisten. Beat the whole egg and egg white together in a small bowl. Add to the meat mixture along with the pepper. Stir to combine the mixture well but be careful not to overwork, or the meat loaf will be tough.

Form into 8 loaves (a heaping $\frac{1}{2}$ cup each) and place in 13 × 9-inch glass baking dish. Spoon the remaining $\frac{1}{4}$ cup Miracle Marinade evenly over the mini meatloaves.

Bake for 25 to 30 minutes. Remove from the oven and spoon the cooking juices in the bottom of the baking dish over the loaves. Cover the top of each loaf with 1 tablespoon Sun-Dried Tomato and Cranberry Ketchup. Return to the oven and bake until the ketchup is glazed, 8 to 10 minutes.

Serves 8

# Crispy Onion-Crusted Steak with Mushroom Cream Sauce

This recipe is inspired by a steak dish my mom used to make, as well as the flavors of an old-fashioned green bean casserole. The combination of crispy onions, tender steak, and creamy sauce give this dish a delicious texture, and the aroma of the mushrooms, garlic, and onions simmering on your stove is sure to get your family excited about dinner.

## MUSHROOM CREAM SAUCE

1 tablespoon unsalted butter

1 tablespoon all-purpose flour

1 cup half-and-half

1/4 cup heavy cream

1/4 teaspoon salt

1/8 teaspoon ground black pepper

1 garlic clove, minced

2 cups chopped baby bella mushrooms (about 6 large)

## STEAK

2 cups canned French-fried onions

1 cup panko breadcrumbs

1/2 cup plus 1 tablespoon all-purpose flour

1/2 teaspoon salt

1/4 teaspoon ground black pepper

3/4 cup buttermilk

4 cube steaks (about 1/4 pound each)

1/4 cup canola or vegetable oil

To make the mushroom cream sauce: Melt the butter in a medium saucepan over medium heat. Add the flour and cook for 1 minute. Whisk in the half-and-half and heavy cream. Stir in the salt, pepper, and garlic and cook for 5 minutes to meld the flavors. Add the mushrooms, reduce the heat to low, and cook for 10 minutes to thicken the sauce and meld the flavors. Remove from the heat and cover to keep warm.

To make the steak: Combine the fried onions, panko, and 1 tablespoon of the flour in a resealable plastic bag. Use a rolling pin to lightly pound the onions until they are crushed. Pour the onion crumbs onto a sheet of wax paper or a plate. Place the remaining 1/2 cup flour, 1/4 of the teaspoon salt, and 1/8 teaspoon of the pepper on a second sheet of wax paper or plate. Pour the buttermilk in a shallow bowl.

Season both sides of cube steaks with the remaining 1/4 teaspoon salt and 1/8 teaspoon pepper. Dredge the steaks in the seasoned flour, then the buttermilk, and then the onion crumbs, pressing them onto the steaks.

Heat the oil in a medium skillet over medium heat. Test the oil to make sure it is hot enough by sprinkling in flour to see if it sizzles. When it sizzles, gently place 2 steaks at a time into the hot oil. Cook on each side for about 2 1/2 minutes. Transfer the steaks to a paper towel–lined plate to drain.

Serve the steaks topped with warm mushroom cream sauce.

Serves 4

# Bacon-Wrapped Sirloin Steak

Filet mignon is my mom's favorite cut of steak, but it's expensive to serve when you're entertaining for a crowd. Sirloin is a much more affordable alternative. Here I have mimicked the filet mignon presentation by wrapping individual sirloin steak rounds in bacon. Soaking the steak in marinade before cooking helps to make the meat even more tender.

2 pounds sirloin steak

1 teaspoon salt

$\frac{1}{4}$ teaspoon ground black pepper

Double recipe Miracle Marinade (page 159)

4 slices bacon

Season the steak on both sides with $\frac{1}{2}$ teaspoon of the salt and $\frac{1}{8}$ teaspoon of the pepper. Place in a shallow dish and pour the marinade over the steak. Cover with plastic wrap and refrigerate for 2 hours.

Preheat the oven to 400°F.

Transfer the steak to a cutting board. Cut steak into 4 rounds. Wrap a slice of bacon around each round. Secure with a toothpick.

Heat a grill pan over medium heat. Coat with cooking spray. Place the steaks on the grill pan and cook for 4 minutes on each side. Transfer the steaks to a baking sheet and bake for 4 minutes for a medium doneness. Transfer to a serving plate to rest for 5 minutes before serving.

Serves 4

# Grandma's Sunday Roast

"Low and slow" is the only way to go, according to my great-grandmother. Her secret method is to cook the roast at a low temperature for 1 hour per pound of meat. One of my secrets for creating a delicious roast is to use an untrimmed bottom round roast; simply ask your butcher if you're unable to find one in the meat case. The fat layer on the roast is key to its succulent flavor. The recipe will feed a large crowd, and leftovers can be used throughout the week for sandwiches like my Mississippi Cheesesteak (page 56).

7- to 8-pound bottom round roast, untrimmed

1 tablespoon garlic salt

1 tablespoon kosher salt

2 teaspoons ground black pepper

2 large yellow onions, thickly sliced

2 cups water

Preheat the oven to 400°F.

Place the roast fat-side down in a roasting pan. Combine the garlic salt, kosher salt, and black pepper in a small bowl. Rub the seasoning over the roast. Top the roast with onion slices.

Pour the water into the bottom of the pan. Cover the roast with foil and bake for 1 hour. Reduce the oven temperature to 250°F. Bake until tender, 6½ to 7 hours.

Remove the roast from oven. Let stand for at least 10 minutes.

Meanwhile, pour the cooking juices out of the roasting pan and skim off the liquid fat. Pour the cooking juices through a strainer into a gravy bowl.

Remove the fat layer from the roast and discard. Place the roast on a serving platter. Pull roast apart or cut into thin slices with an electric knife. Serve the roast with the cooking juices.

Serves 10 to 12

# Summer Vegetable Pizzas

While everyone in my family has his or her own favorite pizza toppings, one thing we all agree on is the more veggies the better! Tomatoes, zucchini, and squash are easy to grow and are usually produced in abundance in the summertime, making them the perfect ingredients for a fresh garden pizza. Feel free to be creative and grill any extra vegetables from your own garden, such as peppers or eggplant.

### TOMATO SAUCE

2 pounds Roma (plum) tomatoes (about 7 large), quartered

5 tablespoons extra-virgin olive oil

$1/2$ teaspoon kosher salt

$1/4$ teaspoon ground black pepper

$1/3$ cup minced yellow onion

2 small carrots, finely grated

2 garlic cloves, minced

1 tablespoon agave nectar

$1/8$ teaspoon table salt

### DOUGH

1 envelope ($1/4$ ounce) active dry yeast

$1 2/3$ cups lukewarm (100° to 110°F) water

4 cups plus 3 tablespoons bread flour

$1/4$ cup plus 3 tablespoons extra-virgin olive oil

$2 1/2$ teaspoons table salt

1 tablespoon yellow cornmeal

Preheat the oven to 400°F.

To make the tomato sauce: Place the tomato pieces on a baking sheet. Drizzle with 4 tablespoons of the oil and sprinkle with the kosher salt and $1/8$ teaspoon of the pepper. Bake until lightly roasted, about 15 minutes.

Meanwhile, heat the remaining 1 tablespoon oil in a medium saucepan. Add the onion and carrot and cook until the onion is translucent and the carrot is softened, about 6 minutes. Add the garlic and cook until fragrant, about 2 minutes.

Transfer the roasted tomatoes to a blender and blend until smooth. Pour into the saucepan with the sautéed vegetables. Stir in the agave nectar and the remaining $1/8$ teaspoon pepper and the table salt. Cover and cook on low until the sauce reaches the desired consistency, 25 to 30 minutes.

To make the dough: In a stand mixer, whisk together the yeast and water. Let stand for 5 minutes. Add the 4 cups flour, the $1/4$ cup oil, and salt. Using a paddle attachment, beat on medium speed until the dough is smooth. Replace the paddle with the dough hook and increase the speed to high. After about 2 minutes, the dough should form and be sticky.

Sprinkle the remaining 3 tablespoons flour on a work surface. Turn the dough out onto the surface and knead in the flour. Form the dough into a smooth ball. Place the dough into lightly oiled bowl and turn to coat. Cover the bowl with plastic wrap and let rise for 1 hour or until doubled in size.

Meanwhile, place an oven rack in the bottom position and preheat to 450°F. About 10 minutes before the dough has doubled in size, put a pizza stone on the bottom rack to preheat.

## GRILLED VEGETABLES

1 small zucchini, cut lengthwise into ¼-inch-thick slices

1 small yellow squash, cut lengthwise into ¼-inch-thick slices

2 small tomatoes, sliced

1 tablespoon extra-virgin olive oil

¼ teaspoon finely chopped fresh rosemary

¼ teaspoon kosher salt

¼ teaspoon ground black pepper

12 ounces fresh mozzarella, sliced

Punch the dough down and divide in half. Place one half of the dough on a floured surface and using a rolling pin, roll out to a round large enough to cover the pizza stone.

Remove the stone from oven and sprinkle with cornmeal. Carefully place the dough round on the stone. Poke a few holes in the dough with a fork. Bake until the dough rises but doesn't brown, about 5 minutes. Remove from the oven. Roll out and bake the second dough round. Leave the oven on.

Meanwhile, grill the vegetables: Combine the zucchini, yellow squash, tomato, oil, rosemary, salt, and pepper in a medium bowl and toss to coat.

Heat a grill pan over medium-high heat. Cook the zucchini and squash slices until grill marks appear, about 1½ minutes on each side. Transfer to a plate. Cook the tomato slices for 45 seconds on each side. Transfer to the plate.

To assemble the pizzas, spread the roasted tomato sauce over the crust. Alternate the grilled zucchini and squash slices over the sauce. Top with the grilled tomato slices.

Bake each pizza for 8 minutes. Remove from the oven and top with the mozzarella. Bake until the cheese has melted, about 5 minutes. Let stand for 5 minutes before using a pizza cutter to cut each pizza into 8 slices.

Serves 6 to 8

··· *6* ···

## SWEET
# REWARDS

I HAVE TO CONFESS that I have a weakness for sweets. I deliberately eat small portions to leave room for dessert. I will make late-night trips to the supermarket just to purchase ingredients for my Molten Lava Cakes to satisfy my chocolate cravings. Deemed the "pastry princess" on *MasterChef,* I spend most of my time in my kitchen, dusted with flour, concocting creations such as Not Your Grandma's Lemon Meringue and Crispy Coconut Bites with Chocolate Sauce.

# Lemon-Lime Fruit Salad

This fresh, citrusy fruit salad is bursting with the flavor of fresh-picked fruit—it's a taste of summer in a bowl! I like to serve it in small portions with lemon-lime whipped cream for a simple, fruity dessert with a special touch. The variety of colored fruits and berries and the petite cut of the fruit make for an especially pretty presentation.

**FRUIT SALAD**

3 tablespoons lemon-lime soda

1 Golden Delicious apple

1 large banana, cut into ¼-inch cubes

2 large navel oranges, peeled and cut into ¼-inch cubes

¼ cup mixed blueberries and blackberries

¼ cup sliced strawberries

3 tablespoons sweetened shredded coconut

1 tablespoon sliced almonds

½ teaspoon honey (optional)

**LEMON-LIME WHIPPED CREAM**

⅔ cup heavy cream, cold

2 tablespoons confectioners' sugar

¼ teaspoon mixed grated lemon and lime zests

To make the fruit salad: Measure the lemon-lime soda into a bowl. Peel and cut the apple into ¼-inch cubes, adding it to the bowl as you work and tossing to coat (to keep the apple from discoloring).

Add the banana, oranges, mixed berries, strawberries, coconut, and almonds and stir gently to combine. If you want more sweetness, stir in the honey. Refrigerate the salad until chilled, at least an 1 hour.

Meanwhile, make the lemon-lime whipped cream: Using an electric mixer, beat the cream until soft peaks form. Sprinkle in the sugar and zest. Beat for about 30 seconds.

Spoon the fruit salad into 6 dessert bowls and top with a dollop of lemon-lime whipped cream.

Serves 6

# Crispy Coconut Bites with Chocolate Sauce

My dad loves the combination of coconut and chocolate. I created this simple dessert using basic, inexpensive pantry ingredients that you probably already have on hand. You'd never guess that the secret ingredient in these decadent little bites is a Southern staple: grits!

### BITES

1⅓ cups canned coconut milk

½ cup quick-cooking grits

3 tablespoons sugar

½ cup heavy cream

⅔ cup graham cracker crumbs

1 cup shredded fresh coconut or packaged sweetened shredded coconut

3 tablespoons unsalted butter

### CHOCOLATE SAUCE

¼ cup heavy cream

4 ounces good-quality semisweet chocolate, coarsely chopped

To make the bites: Bring the coconut milk to a slight boil in a small saucepan over medium-high heat. Whisk in the grits and reduce the heat to low. Cook, stirring occasionally, until the grits reach porridge consistency, about 5 minutes. Remove from the heat and stir in the sugar. Scrape into a small bowl and let cool at room temperature, about 25 minutes.

Scooping 1 tablespoon of grits at a time, gently roll the mixture with the palms of your hands to form 12 balls. Place the balls on a plastic wrap–covered baking sheet. The balls can be made up several hours ahead of time.

Pour the cream into a shallow dish. Place the graham cracker crumbs and shredded coconut on two separate plates. Roll the grit balls in the cream, then the crumbs, back into the cream, and then the coconut.

Melt 1 tablespoon of the butter in a small heavy nonstick pan over medium-high heat. Cook 4 balls until lightly browned all over, a few seconds on each side. Transfer the balls to a paper towel–lined plate. Wipe the pan clean and repeat with the remaining butter and grits balls, using 1 tablespoon of butter for each batch.

To make the chocolate sauce: Heat the cream in a small saucepan over medium-high heat until it begins to boil. Place the chocolate in a heatproof bowl. Pour the hot cream over the chocolate and stir until smooth.

Serve the crispy coconut bites with the chocolate sauce.

*Serves 6*

# No-Name Bars

There's an old saying that you can never have too much chocolate. Well, for me, you can never have too much cream cheese! I call these No-Name Bars because they're really too good for words. You can top these cheesecake-like squares with any fruit you want (or even chocolate sauce). I like to serve mine topped with fresh cooked cherries.

**CRUST**

1½ sticks (6 ounces) unsalted butter, melted

¾ cup granulated sugar

1½ cups all-purpose flour

½ teaspoon baking powder

½ teaspoon baking soda

½ teaspoon salt

1 teaspoon vanilla extract

**FILLING**

1 package (8 ounces) cream cheese, at room temperature

2 large eggs

4 tablespoons (½ stick) unsalted butter, melted

1 teaspoon pure vanilla extract

3½ cups confectioners' sugar

Preheat the oven to 350°F. Grease 13 × 9-inch baking dish.

To make the crust: Mix the melted butter and granulated sugar together in a medium bowl. In another bowl, mix the flour, baking powder, baking soda, and salt. Add the flour mixture to the butter mixture and mix until combined. Stir in the vanilla. Spread the mixture into bottom of the baking dish.

To make the filling: Beat the cream cheese with an electric mixer until smooth. Add the eggs and mix until combined. Stir in the melted butter and vanilla. Stir in the confectioners' sugar. Spread the mixture on top of the crust.

Bake until set, about 38 minutes. Let cool for 5 minutes before cutting into squares.

Serves 8

# Sweet Potato Peanut Butter Blondies

Anyone traveling through Mississippi is likely to see a pickup truck along the side of the highway filled with sweet potatoes for sale. With sweet potatoes being so plentiful, I am always trying to come up with new ways to use them in my cooking and baking. This recipe combines my love of three things: sweet potatoes, blondies, and peanut butter!

Unsalted butter, for greasing baking dish

2 cups sifted all-purpose flour

1 teaspoon baking powder

1 teaspoon salt

$\frac{1}{4}$ teaspoon baking soda

$\frac{2}{3}$ cup unsalted butter, melted

2 cups packed light brown sugar

2 large eggs, lightly beaten

1 cup cooked and mashed sweet potato

$\frac{2}{3}$ cup peanut butter

2 tablespoons pure vanilla extract

$\frac{1}{8}$ teaspoon ground cinnamon

Preheat the oven to 350°F. Grease a 13 × 9-inch baking pan with unsalted butter.

Sift together the flour, baking powder, salt, and baking soda into a small bowl.

In a medium bowl, mix together the melted butter and brown sugar. Stir in the beaten eggs, sweet potato, peanut butter, vanilla, and cinnamon until combined. Add the flour mixture ingredients and mix well.

Spread the batter evenly in the baking dish. Bake for 18 minutes. Let cool for 10 minutes. Cut the blondies into squares or desired shapes.

Serves 8 to 10

# Strawberry Cream Cupcakes

Birthdays are a big deal in my family. Each birthday girl or boy gets to request his or her own favorite cake for the day. My mom's favorite is German chocolate. I like coconut with lemon cream filling. My sister Brittyn loves strawberry cream cake. In fact she loves it so much that I have nicknamed it "Brittyn's birthday cake." This is the cupcake version of Brittyn's much-loved cake. Once your friends and family have tasted these fluffy, creamy cupcakes, don't be surprised if they start requesting them for their birthdays, too!

1 box (16 ounces) angel food cake mix

1 package (8 ounces) cream cheese, at room temperature

1 cup sweetened condensed milk

1 cup sliced strawberries plus 15 slices for garnish

2 cups heavy cream, cold

5 tablespoons confectioners' sugar

Preheat the oven to 350°F. Line a 6-cup jumbo muffin tin with paper liners.

Prepare the angel food cake batter according to package directions. Fill the paper liners three-quarters of the way to the top with batter. Bake until the cupcakes just start to turn golden brown, 15 to 17 minutes. Remove the cupcakes from the pan and transfer to a rack to cool completely. Let the muffin tin cool and repeat for 2 more batches (the last batch will only be 3 cupcakes).

Using an electric mixer, beat the cream cheese in a medium bowl until smooth. Beat in the condensed milk. Fold in the 1 cup strawberries. Refrigerate until it firms up, about 40 minutes.

Once the filling has firmed up and the cupcakes have cooled completely, carefully cut off the cupcake tops with a sharp knife and set aside. Make a slit in the top of each cupcake with a sharp knife and push down on the airy cake to make a 1-inch-deep well. Fill the well with the strawberry filling using a small spoon. Replace the cupcake tops, pressing lightly to seal.

Beat the cream in a cold bowl with an electric mixer until soft peaks form. Beat in the confectioners' sugar until combined. Fill a resealable plastic bag with the whipped cream and snip off the corner of the bag.

Pipe the whipped cream onto the tops of the cupcakes in a circular motion. Top with a strawberry slice. Serve immediately or refrigerate until ready to serve.

Makes 15 jumbo cupcakes

# Toasted Coconut Cupcakes
# with Lemon Glaze

When I was under pressure to create a perfect cupcake on *MasterChef*, my mind immediately went back to my inspiration: My 95-year-old great-grandmother and her wonderful homemade cake with a lemon glaze. This cupcake recipe infuses a moist yellow cake with coconut flavor and is topped with a light, tangy lemon glaze and crunchy toasted coconut.

## CUPCAKES

1¼ cups cake flour

1 teaspoon baking powder

½ teaspoon baking soda

¼ teaspoon salt

8 tablespoons (1 stick) unsalted butter, at room temperature

1 cup sugar

1 large egg plus 2 large egg yolks, lightly beaten, at room temperature

½ cup whole milk

1 teaspoon canned coconut water

½ teaspoon pure vanilla extract

## TOPPING

1 cup sweetened shredded coconut

## LEMON GLAZE

³⁄₈ teaspoon grated lemon zest

2 teaspoons fresh lemon juice

1 cup confectioners' sugar

Preheat the oven to 350°F. Line the cups of one 12-cup muffin tin and 4 cups of a second 12-cup muffin tin with paper liners.

To make the cupcakes: Sift together the flour, baking powder, baking soda, and salt in a small bowl.

Place the butter in a large bowl and stir until it reaches a creamy consistency. Slowly stir the sugar into butter. Slowly stir in the egg mixture. Add one-third of the flour mixture. Add one-half of the milk. Continue adding them alternately, ending with the flour mixture. Stir the batter after each addition. Stir in the coconut water and vanilla.

Fill the paper liners half full of batter. Bake until a toothpick inserted in the center of a cupcake comes out clean, about 14 minutes. Leave the oven on. Transfer the cupcakes to a rack to cool, about 20 minutes.

To make the topping: Spread the coconut on a baking sheet and bake lightly browned and fragrant, 7 to 8 minutes. Transfer to a shallow bowl and let cool.

To make the lemon glaze: Mix together the lemon zest, lemon juice, 2 tablespoons water, and confectioners' sugar in a small shallow bowl.

To assemble, dip the top of a cooled cupcake in the glaze. Immediately dip the glazed top in the coconut. Allow the glaze to set before serving or storing the cupcakes.

Makes 16 cupcakes

# Molten Lava Cakes for a Crowd

Rich and fudgy brownies were the go-to dessert at my house when a chocolate craving struck. That is, until I started making my molten lava cakes. These rich, gooey cakes will satisfy even the most die-hard chocoholics, and since they're baked in a muffin tin, it's easy to whip up a large batch in no time at all.

**WHIPPED CREAM**

1 cup heavy cream, cold

2½ tablespoons confectioners' sugar

**CAKES**

1 cup dark chocolate chips

1 stick plus 2 tablespoons (5 ounces) unsalted butter

2 tablespoons brewed coffee

½ cup all-purpose flour

1½ cups confectioners' sugar

3 large eggs, lightly beaten

3 large egg yolks, lightly beaten

1 teaspoon pure vanilla extract

2 tablespoons unsweetened cocoa powder

Preheat the oven to 400°F. Lightly coat a 12-cup muffin tin with cooking spray.

To make the whipped cream: Beat the cream using an electric mixer in a large cold bowl until soft peaks form. Gradually beat in 2 tablespoons of the confectioner' sugar. Cover and refrigerate while you make the cakes.

To make the cakes: Melt the chocolate chips and butter in a medium saucepan over low heat, stirring frequently. Once the chocolate and butter are melted, stir in the coffee until smooth.

In a medium bowl, sift together the flour and confectioners' sugar. Stir in the chocolate mixture. Add the whole eggs and egg yolks one at a time, beating well after each addition. Stir in the vanilla.

Divide the batter evenly among the muffin cups. Bake until the cakes are slightly jiggly in the center, about 7 minutes. Run a butter knife around the edges of each cake and transfer the hot cakes to dessert plates. Top with a dollop of whipped cream and dust with the cocoa powder.

Serves 12

# Not Your Grandma's Lemon Meringue

On Sunday morning, my grandma would often whip up a "few" (at least three or more) lemon meringue pies for Sunday dinner. Although the taste of this tangy lemon dessert transports me back to my grandma's kitchen, it's actually a very different dessert comprised of four separate elements: lemon panna cotta, lemon curd, meringue shell, and tuile cookies. You can make each of these components ahead of time and assemble it for your guests at the last minute.

## MERINGUE SHELLS

3 large egg whites, at room temperature

½ teaspoon pure vanilla extract

¼ teaspoon cream of tartar

½ cup superfine sugar*

## PANNA COTTA

1 cup half-and-half

1 cup whole milk

1½ teaspoons grated lemon zest

1½ teaspoons unflavored gelatin powder

¼ cup superfine sugar*

## TUILE COOKIES

2 large egg whites, at room temperature

½ cup sifted confectioners' sugar

½ cup sifted all-purpose flour

3 tablespoons unsalted butter, melted

¼ teaspoon pure vanilla extract

*If you do not have superfine sugar, pulse granulated sugar two times in a food processor.*

Preheat the oven to 225°F.

To make the meringues: Line a baking sheet with parchment paper. Using a pencil, trace four 4-inch circles on the paper using a glass or cookie cutter as a guide. Turn the paper drawing-side down.

In a stand mixer, beat the egg whites, vanilla, and cream of tartar on medium speed until soft peaks form. Reduce to low speed and gradually beat in the superfine sugar. Once all the sugar is incorporated, increase the speed to high and beat until stiff peaks form.

Spoon the meringue onto each parchment paper circle, smoothing the meringue to make a solid round. To make the shells, use the back of a spoon to push the meringue toward the edge of the round to form a 1-inch-high wall. Swirl meringue up into short peaks on the sides.

Bake until firm, about 1 hour. Turn the oven off and leave the meringues in the turned-off oven for 1 hour.

To make the panna cotta: Heat ¾ cup of the half-and-half and the milk in a heavy medium saucepan over medium heat. Add the zest and cook for 8 minutes to infuse the mixture with lemon zest flavor.

Meanwhile, pour the remaining ¼ cup half-and-half into a shallow bowl. Sprinkle the gelatin over the half-and-half and let stand for 10 minutes.

Stir the superfine sugar into the milk mixture in the saucepan, whisking to dissolve. Remove from the heat and stir in the softened gelatin, whisking until it dissolves. If any gelatin particles remain, return to low heat and stir until it's all dissolved.

*(continued on page 132)*

## LEMON CURD

¼ cup plus 2 tablespoons
    granulated sugar

¼ teaspoon grated lemon zest

¼ cup fresh lemon juice

1 large egg yolk

1 teaspoon unsalted butter, at room
    temperature

## SWEETENED BLACKBERRIES

¾ cup blackberries

2 tablespoons turbinado sugar

Grease four 3-inch ramekins or 4 cups of a muffin tin. Strain the milk mixture through a fine-mesh sieve into a large measuring bowl or container for easy pouring. Fill the ramekins or cups. Cover with plastic wrap and refrigerate until set, 2 to 4 hours.

To make the tuile cookies: Whisk the egg whites in a bowl. Whisk in the confectioners' sugar until smooth. Whisk in the flour to combine. Stir in the melted butter and vanilla. Whisk until smooth. Cover and refrigerate for 30 minutes.

Preheat the oven to 350°F. Line a baking sheet with a nonstick liner or parchment paper.

Working quickly, spoon no more than ½ teaspoon batter onto the prepared baking sheet to form thin cookies. Using the back of a spoon or offset spatula, thinly spread the batter into rounds. Bake until lightly browned around the edges, 3 to 5 minutes. Quickly use a spatula to remove the cookies from the baking sheet. While hot and soft, mold the cookies over a wooden spoon handle or rolling pin to form curved shapes.

To make the lemon curd: Heat the granulated sugar, lemon zest, and lemon juice in a small heavy saucepan over medium heat, stirring until the sugar dissolves. Remove from the heat and quickly whisk in the egg yolk. Return to the heat and cook, stirring constantly, until the mixture slightly thickens, 8 to 10 minutes. Remove from the heat and strain through a fine-mesh sieve into a small bowl. Stir in the butter until it melts. Cover the surface of the curd with plastic wrap to keep a skin from forming. Refrigerate until firmed up, about 10 minutes.

To prepare the sweetened blackberries: Combine the blackberries, turbinado sugar, and ½ cup water in a small heavy saucepan. Cook over medium heat, stirring constantly, until the sugar dissolves, about 4 minutes. Remove from the heat and set aside.

To assemble, place a meringue shell on a dessert plate. Unmold a panna cotta into the shell. Spoon about 1 tablespoon lemon curd in a line down the side of the plate. Using the back of a spoon, widen the line to a pretty smear. Top the panna cotta with a tuile cookie. Lastly, spoon a few blackberries around the meringue shell. Drop a few dots of blackberry juice onto the lemon curd for decoration.

Serves 4

# White Chocolate Bread Pudding

Bread pudding is a popular ending to many Southern meals. As delicious as it may be, sometimes bread pudding can feel like a heavy dessert. My recipe uses light, airy French bread, which keeps the texture of the pudding from becoming too dense. I love the combination of creamy custard and warm white chocolate sauce—and so will your guests!

## BREAD PUDDING

7 ounces French bread, crusts removed and cut into 1-inch cubes (8 cups)

3 large eggs

7 large egg yolks

1/2 cup plus 2 tablespoons sugar

3 1/2 cups half-and-half

1 cup plus 2 tablespoons heavy cream

1 cup good-quality white chocolate chips

1 tablespoon pure vanilla extract

## WHITE CHOCOLATE SAUCE

1 cup good-quality white chocolate chips

1 1/2 cups heavy cream

Preheat the oven to 350°F. Grease a 13 × 9-inch glass baking dish.

To make the bread pudding: Place the bread cubes on a baking sheet and bake until golden brown, 8 to 10 minutes. Transfer to the baking dish.

Whisk together the whole eggs, egg yolks, and sugar in a large bowl.

Combine the half-and-half and 1 cup of the heavy cream in a medium saucepan. Heat over medium heat until hot, about 7 minutes. Whisking constantly, slowly add hot milk mixture to the egg mixture.

Melt the white chocolate with the remaining 2 tablespoons heavy cream in a small saucepan over low heat. Pour the white chocolate into the egg mixture, stirring occasionally. Stir in the vanilla.

Strain the mixture through a fine-mesh sieve over the bread cubes. Lightly press the cubes into the milk mixture to submerge them. Bake until the bread has absorbed the liquid and is lightly toasted, about 40 minutes. Let stand for 5 minutes before serving.

To make the white chocolate sauce: Melt the chocolate with the cream in a medium saucepan over low heat, stirring occasionally.

Serve the bread pudding warm with white chocolate sauce drizzled over the top.

Serves 8 to 10

# Banana Mousse Trifles

Sunday dinners at my Grandma's house often included homemade banana pudding for dessert. This recipe captures the rich flavor of her original dish with a lighter, creamier texture. You can make the mousse a day ahead and assemble the trifle just before serving.

## MOUSSE

½ cup plus 2 tablespoons
    granulated sugar

¼ cup cornstarch

Pinch of salt

3 large eggs, separated

2 cups fat-free milk

2 teaspoons pure vanilla extract

Juice of ½ orange

1 large banana

1½ cups heavy cream, cold

1 box (12 ounces) vanilla wafers
    (you may not need all of them)

## WHIPPED CREAM

½ cup heavy cream, cold

4 teaspoons confectioners' sugar

To make the mousse: Mix ½ cup of the granulated sugar, the cornstarch, and salt in a medium bowl. Stir in the egg yolks and ½ cup of the milk.

Heat the remaining 1½ cups milk in a medium saucepan over medium heat until the milk is hot but not boiling, about 3 minutes. Whisking constantly, gradually beat the hot milk into the egg mixture. Pour the mixture back into the saucepan and cook over medium heat, stirring constantly, for 4 minutes. Pour into a heatproof bowl. Stir in the vanilla. Cover the surface of the pudding with plastic wrap to keep a skin from forming. Refrigerate until set, about 1 hour.

Place the orange juice in a small bowl. Slice the banana and toss the slices with the orange juice. Pat bananas dry with paper towel and puree in a food processor. Stir the banana puree into the chilled pudding.

Beat the egg whites with an electric mixer in a medium bowl until they form soft peaks. Fold the beaten whites into the banana pudding.

Beat the cream with an electric mixer in a cold bowl until soft peaks form. Gradually beat in the remaining 2 tablespoons granulated sugar. Fold the cream into the banana pudding. Cover with plastic wrap and refrigerate until chilled, about 30 minutes.

Preheat the oven to 375°F. Place as many vanilla wafers as will fit on a baking sheet and bake until lightly toasted, about 3 minutes.

To whip the cream: Beat the cream with an electric mixer in a small cold bowl until soft peaks form. Gradually beat in the confectioners' sugar.

To assemble mini trifles, place a toasted vanilla wafer into the bottom of a small glass or parfait dish. Spoon 1 or 2 tablespoons banana mousse on top. Continue layering wafers and mousse, ending with mousse. Top with a dollop of whipped cream and a final wafer.

Serves 8

# Southern Affogato

Whenever I can, I like to use local ingredients in my recipes. I enjoy going to a nearby farm and picking up my own pecans, bringing them home, cracking the shells, and extracting the "nut meat." Then the cooking can begin . . . pecan pies, brownies, cookies, and yes, homemade ice cream. My butter pecan ice cream makes a wonderful topping for any dessert and is delicious when paired with steaming hot espresso. The recipe below makes 1½ quarts—roughly double what you'll need to make 6 affogatos. But if you're going to the trouble of making homemade ice cream for your guests, you'll want some left over for yourself!

**BUTTER PECAN ICE CREAM**
2 tablespoons unsalted butter
½ cup chopped pecans
3 large eggs
¾ cup packed light brown sugar
¼ teaspoon salt
1½ cups heavy cream*
1½ cups half-and-half
2 teaspoons pure vanilla extract

**AFFOGATO**
6 shots of freshly brewed espresso

*For a lighter version, substitute whole milk for the heavy cream.*

To make the ice cream: Melt the butter in a small skillet over medium heat. Stir in the pecans and cook, stirring occasionally, until lightly toasted, 2 to 3 minutes. Set aside.

Whisk the eggs in a medium bowl. Stir in the brown sugar and salt. Set aside.

Combine the cream and half-and-half in a medium saucepan. Cook over medium heat until the liquid starts to simmer, 3 to 5 minutes. Remove from the heat. Whisking constantly, stir a few spoonfuls of hot cream into the egg mixture to warm it. Whisking briskly, gradually beat the warmed eggs into the hot cream in the saucepan. Return to the heat and cook over medium-low until the custard thickens, about 9 minutes. The custard should coat the back of the spoon.

Remove from the heat and stir in the vanilla and pecans. Pour into a bowl and refrigerate until well chilled, 1 to 2 hours. Pour into an ice-cream maker and freeze according to the manufacturer's directions.

For each serving of affogato: Place a scoop of ice cream in 6 small bowls and top with a shot of steaming hot espresso. Serve immediately.

Serve 6

# Vanilla Rice Pudding

When my mom was a little girl, her mother used to cook rice pudding—a frugal dessert made from leftover cooked rice. My more modern version of this homespun dessert is made with jasmine rice, whipping cream, and vanilla bean. At my house, we often top it with fresh fruit and nuts. Sometimes, I might even sprinkle sugar on top and brûlée it.

1 cup cooked jasmine rice

1½ cups fat-free milk

½ cup heavy cream

½ cup granulated sugar

⅛ teaspoon salt

1 vanilla bean (split lengthwise and scraped), 1 tablespoon vanilla bean paste, or 2 teaspoons pure vanilla extract

1 large egg

1 large egg yolk

1 tablespoon unsalted butter

Heat the rice, milk, cream, sugar, and salt in a saucepan over medium-low heat, stirring until the sugar dissolves. Add the vanilla bean and seeds. Reduce heat to low and cook, stirring occasionally, until thickened, about 15 minutes. Remove from the heat. Discard the bean.

Beat the whole egg and egg yolk in a small bowl. Stir in a few tablespoons of the hot milk mixture into the eggs to warm them. Slowly mix the warmed eggs back into the saucepan. Return the saucepan to low heat and cook, stirring constantly, for 5 minutes. Remove from heat and stir in the butter. Let cool for 5 minutes.

Serve the pudding warm or pour into a bowl, refrigerate for 1 to 2 hours, and serve chilled.

Serves 4 to 6

Taking the time to gather and arrange flowers in season for the dinner table—even during the week—gives an air of elegance to the meal. It also gives the cook a reason to get outside!

7

## CHIC
# SIPS

I ALWAYS LIKE TO SERVE MY GUESTS creative, playful, and delicious drinks. Whether it is the citrusy scent of a tangerine slice perched on the rim of the glass of sweet tangerine tea or the sweet and crispy combination of honey and toasted coconut on the rim of my mocktail Pineapple Coolada, small accents make these chic sips a refreshing sensory experience that will delight family and friends.

# Tangerine Tea

Sweet tea is considered a necessity at my house. I grew up in a household where dinner was accompanied by sweet tea by the gallon! Usually a glass of iced tea is served with fresh lemon, but I think that the flavor of tangerine is even better. When I served a glass to my mom with a tangerine slice perched on the rim, she was in love with the fragrance before she even took a sip.

1 or 2 black tea bags of choice

$3/4$ cup sugar

4 tangerine slices, plus additional
    for garnish

Bring 2 cups water to a boil in a medium saucepan over medium-high heat. Add the tea bag(s) and boil for 2 minutes. Remove from the heat.

Combine $3/4$ cup water and the sugar in a small saucepan. Bring to a simmer over medium-low heat, stirring constantly until the sugar dissolves. Place the tangerine slices in the sugar syrup. Reduce the heat to medium-low and cook for 4 minutes to infuse the syrup with tangerine flavor.

Squeeze the tea bag and discard. Discard the tangerine slices. Pour the tangerine syrup into the pan of tea and stir.

Combine the tangerine tea and 2 cups water in a glass pitcher. Stir together until combined. Serve over ice with a tangerine slice hooked on the rim of the glass.

Serves 4

# Hot Chocolate with Agave Marshmallows

Growing up, my great-grandma used to make real hot chocolate by slowly mixing cocoa powder, sugar, and milk in a large pot on the stove. Today, my family still enjoys a cup of hot chocolate in the wintertime, especially when we get home late at night after a ballgame. Drinking a rich, creamy cup of cocoa with homemade marshmallows seems to warm us up from the inside out.

6 ounces 70% cacao chocolate, coarsely chopped

1/4 cup turbinado sugar

1/8 teaspoon salt

1/2 cup boiling water

2 1/2 cups fat-free milk

2 cups whole milk

1/2 teaspoon pure vanilla extract

8 Agave Marshmallows (recipe on opposite page)

Combine the chocolate, sugar, and salt in a medium saucepan. Stir in the boiling water until the chocolate and sugar melt. Bring the mixture to a slight boil over medium-high heat, stirring occasionally. Stir in both milks and heat until hot. Remove from the heat and stir in the vanilla. Serve with marshmallows.

Serves 4

When you're having guests over, jazz up the drinks you're serving by using colorful glassware and mugs. Rim the glasses with ingredients like colored sugar, finely ground cookie crumbs, or spices such as cocoa powder or cinnamon for an extra special touch. Rock candy on a stick makes a great stirrer, too!

# Agave Marshmallows

1½ tablespoons cornstarch

2 envelopes unflavored gelatin

¼ teaspoon stevia powder

¾ cup light agave nectar

⅛ teaspoon salt

1 teaspoon pure vanilla extract

Lightly coat the bottom of a 13 × 9 × 2-inch pan with cooking spray. Line the bottom of the pan with parchment paper. Sift enough cornstarch over the bottom of the pan to lightly but evenly coat.

Sprinkle the gelatin over ½ cup cold water in a small saucepan. Stir over low heat until dissolved. Add the stevia, agave, and salt. Mix well, then heat over medium-high heat until it almost comes to a boil.

Pour the warm syrup into the bowl of a stand mixer. Beat on high speed until the mixture has doubled in volume and forms stiff peaks, about 15 minutes. Beat in the vanilla.

Scrape the marshmallow cream into the prepared pan and spread with a damp rubber spatula. Let stand, uncovered, until set, at least 3 hours.

To make cubes, dip a knife in hot water and cut the marshmallow into 2-inch cubes.

Makes about 50 marshmallows

# Sweet and Tart Lemonade

"Real" lemonade made with fresh lemon juice is always worth the effort. I think my recipe captures the perfect balance of sweetness and tartness. This refreshing drink is delicious anytime, though I especially like pairing it with a salad or dessert.

1 cup sugar

1 cup fresh lemon juice (5 to 6 lemons), plus 2 or 3 lemon slices (for garnish)

Fresh mint leaves (optional)

Combine 1 cup water and the sugar in a saucepan. Bring to a simmer over medium-low heat, stirring constantly until the sugar dissolves. Pour into a container and refrigerate until chilled.

Pour the lemon juice into a pitcher and add the sugar syrup. Add 4 cups water and stir well. Float 2 or 3 lemon slices in the pitcher for extra lemon flavor.

Serve over ice and garnish the glasses with fresh mint, if desired.

Serves 4 to 6

# Party Punch

This recipe was inspired by one of the South's most famous punches, Planter's Punch. Legend has it that the recipe was first created in the 19th century at the Planter's Hotel in Charleston, South Carolina. This "virgin" punch is perfect for any occasion—from children's birthday parties to more formal evening gatherings. Not only is this pink, fruity punch refreshing and delicious, but it also looks stunning when served in a glass punch bowl.

4 cups orange juice

4 cups pineapple juice

2 cups grenadine

2 cups ice

1 cup fresh orange segments, halved

1 cup fresh pineapple cubes

1 cup club soda

7 fresh mint leaves—4 very thinly sliced, 3 left whole

In a large bowl, stir together the orange juice, pineapple juice, and grenadine. Refrigerate until cold, 1 to 2 hours.

When ready to serve, transfer the chilled fruit juice and grenadine mixture to a punch bowl. Add the ice, fresh fruit, club soda, and sliced mint. Stir to combine.

Garnish the punch bowl with the whole mint leaves.

Serves 10 to 12

# Pineapple Coolada

Steamy temperatures in the South call for a cool and refreshing drink, whether it be for a party or simply a summertime treat, so I created my version of a piña colada. Using fresh fruit takes the guilt out of the indulgence. This drink is always a favorite among adults and kids alike.

¼ cup graham cracker crumbs

¼ cup grated fresh coconut

4 cups cubed fresh pineapple

16 cubes (1 inch) fresh coconut

¼ cup fresh coconut water

¼ cup pineapple juice

2 tablespoons plus 2 teaspoons superfine sugar

4 cups ice

2 teaspoons honey

Preheat the oven to 400°F. Spread the graham cracker crumbs and coconut on a baking sheet and bake until toasted, about 4 minutes. Transfer to a shallow bowl.

Working in batches (depending on the size of your blender), combine the pineapple cubes, coconut cubes, coconut water, pineapple juice, sugar, and ice in a blender. Blend until smooth.

Rim the edges of 4 stemmed glasses with honey. Twist the honey-rimmed glasses in the toasted graham cracker and coconut mixture. Pour the drink into the glasses.

Serves 4

··· *8* ···

# WHITNEY'S
# ESSENTIALS

I HAVE A FEW RECIPES that I just can't do without. If I'd had a secret stash of my Miracle Marinade for the burger challenge on *MasterChef,* the votes would have piled in. I can take any cut of meat and create fantastic flavor with it. Whether drizzled over my Off-the-Griddle Cheeseburger or Mini Meat Loaves, my Sundried Tomato and Cranberry Ketchup is another essential recipe in my repetoire. I like to make these simple, satisfying, and endlessly versatile recipes ahead of time in multiple batches so I always have enough on hand.

Blackened Seasoning Rub
• 158 •

Miracle Marinade
• 159 •

Buttermilk Herb Dressing
• 160 •

Sun-Dried Tomato and
Cranberry Ketchup
• 161 •

Olive Salad
• 162 •

Pimiento Cheese
• 163 •

Turnip Greens Pesto
• 164 •

# Blackened Seasoning Rub

New Orleans is a short drive from my hometown, so my family often makes day trips there to shop at the French Market, eat beignets at Café Du Monde, and sample Creole and Cajun cuisine, which includes a variety of "blackened" seafood. I've created my own blackened seasoning blend that I use at home to cook everything from shrimp to catfish.

2 teaspoons garlic powder

1 teaspoon chili powder

1 teaspoon onion powder

$\frac{1}{2}$ teaspoon ground cumin

$\frac{1}{2}$ teaspoon paprika

$\frac{1}{2}$ teaspoon salt

$\frac{1}{4}$ teaspoon cayenne pepper

$\frac{1}{4}$ teaspoon ground black pepper

Combine all the ingredients in a small bowl and blend well. Use immediately or store in an airtight container for 3 to 4 months.

Makes $2\frac{1}{2}$ tablespoons

# Miracle Marinade

As a fan of cooking competitions, I've spent many an afternoon cheering on the creators of prize-winning burgers. Every cook has his or her secret to the perfect burger—and this is mine. My Miracle Marinade transforms ordinary burgers, meat loaf, and even steak into blue-ribbon dishes. The recipe will be our little secret!

1 teaspoon extra-virgin olive oil

4 teaspoons finely diced onion

$\frac{1}{2}$ cup soy sauce

2 teaspoons apple cider vinegar

2 teaspoons fresh lime juice

2 teaspoons orange juice

$\frac{1}{2}$ teaspoon minced garlic

$\frac{1}{4}$ teaspoon minced fresh ginger

2 teaspoons sugar

$\frac{1}{2}$ teaspoon paprika

Heat a small skillet over medium-low heat. Add the oil and onion. Cook until tender and caramelized, 2 to 4 minutes.

Combine the remaining ingredients in a small bowl. Stir in the caramelized onions until well combined.

Use immediately or store in an airtight container in the refrigerator for up to 1 week.

Makes $\frac{1}{2}$ cup

# Buttermilk Herb Dressing

My dad loves ranch dressing—but only if it's fresh and homemade. If we go to a restaurant that doesn't offer real ranch dressing, he simply won't order a salad! My homemade buttermilk herb dressing is his favorite variety of "ranch." You can double or even triple the herb mix and store it in an airtight container for future use so you can always whip up a quick batch of dressing. Once you realize how easy it is to make your own dressing, you'll never buy the bottled stuff again!

**HERB MIX**

2 tablespoons instant nonfat dry milk

1 tablespoon dried parsley flakes

$\frac{1}{2}$ teaspoon dried chives

$\frac{1}{2}$ teaspoon dried dill weed

$\frac{1}{2}$ teaspoon garlic powder

$\frac{1}{2}$ teaspoon onion powder

$\frac{1}{4}$ teaspoon Worcestershire and black pepper blend

$\frac{1}{4}$ teaspoon cayenne pepper

$\frac{1}{4}$ teaspoon salt

$\frac{1}{8}$ teaspoon paprika

**DRESSING**

1 cup mayonnaise

1 cup buttermilk

$\frac{1}{2}$ teaspoon fresh lemon juice

To make the herb mix: Combine all of the ingredients in a small bowl. For a spicy variation, try adding $\frac{1}{4}$ teaspoon each cumin and chili powder and $\frac{1}{8}$ teaspoon cayenne pepper to the herb mix.

To make the dressing: Whisk together the mayonnaise, buttermilk, and lemon juice. Add the herb mix and stir to combine well. Transfer the contents to a bottle with a resealable lid. Refrigerate for at least 30 minutes before using and shake well before serving. The dressing will keep in the fridge for about a week.

Makes 2 cups

# Sun-Dried Tomato and Cranberry Ketchup

Ketchup is a great pantry staple for adding flavor to a variety of vegetable and meat dishes. But ever since I created this recipe, the bottle of ketchup in our pantry has been replaced for good! The cranberries and sun-dried tomatoes add a depth of flavor you just can't find on the supermarket shelf.

3 vine-ripened tomatoes, chopped

15 grape tomatoes, halved

3 tablespoons diced red onion

3 heaping tablespoons dried cranberries

2 tablespoons diced oil-packed sun-dried tomatoes (about 4 whole)

1 garlic clove, minced

1 tablespoon plus $\frac{1}{2}$ teaspoon light brown sugar

1 teaspoon balsamic vinegar

$\frac{1}{2}$ teaspoon apple cider vinegar

$\frac{1}{4}$ teaspoon salt

Splash of lemon juice

Combine all the ingredients with 3 tablespoons water in a medium saucepan. Cook over medium heat for 10 minutes. Reduce the heat to low and cook for 15 minutes to blend the flavors. Let cool for 15 minutes.

Pour the mixture into a food processor and process until almost smooth. Strain the mixture through a fine-mesh sieve into a medium bowl. Refrigerate for 1 hour before use. Store in the refrigerator in an airtight container.

Makes about 2 cups

# Olive Salad

Although typically used in muffuletta sandwiches, this olive salad can also be served with olive oil and Rosemary Focaccia (page 81) for a simple appetizer. You can also try tossing it with pasta and diced vegetables or shrimp to create a Cajun-style pasta salad.

1 jar (16 ounces) giardiniera (marinated mixed vegetables)

6 ounces pitted black olives, such as kalamatas

1 jar (5.5 ounces) pitted Spanish green olives, drained

2 tablespoons extra-virgin olive oil

$\frac{1}{2}$ teaspoon capers

$\frac{1}{4}$ teaspoon grated garlic

$\frac{1}{2}$ teaspoon dried oregano

$\frac{1}{2}$ teaspoon ground black pepper

$\frac{1}{8}$ teaspoon paprika

Pinch of cayenne pepper

Place all the ingredients in a food processor and pulse on and off until coarsely pureed. Use immediately or store in an airtight container in the refrigerator for 1 week.

Makes 4 cups

# Pimiento Cheese

A favorite church potluck dish is a plate of petite pimiento cheese sandwiches. Church potlucks have long been a tradition in the South, and they provide a wonderful opportunity for fellowship—and trying new dishes! I've created two variations of pimiento cheese; the spicy version works well in both hot and cold dishes. The plain version is best in hot dishes—and has the added benefit of being lower in fat and calories.

## SPICY

$\frac{1}{4}$ cup cream cheese, at room temperature

1 cup shredded pepper Jack cheese

$\frac{1}{2}$ cup shredded Cheddar cheese

3 tablespoons mayonnaise

1 tablespoon chopped pimientos

$\frac{1}{8}$ teaspoon salt

$\frac{1}{8}$ teaspoon ground black pepper

Pinch of cayenne pepper

## PLAIN

4 ounces ricotta cheese

$\frac{3}{4}$ cup shredded mozzarella cheese

$\frac{3}{4}$ cup shredded sharp Cheddar cheese

2 tablespoons mayonnaise

1 tablespoon chopped pimientos

Pinch of salt

$\frac{1}{8}$ teaspoon cracked black pepper

Depending on which cheese you are making, first process the cream or ricotta cheese until smooth. Transfer to a medium bowl and stir in the remaining ingredients until combined.

Makes about $1\frac{1}{2}$ cups

# Turnip Greens Pesto

For a quick appetizer that only takes minutes to prepare, try serving this pesto with fresh-baked Cornbread Crostini (page 22), or Rosemary Focaccia Bread (page 81). I also like to use this fresh, bright-tasting pesto sauce as a replacement for condiments like mayonnaise and salad dressing in pasta salads such as Turnip Greens Pesto Pasta Salad (page 80).

11 turnip green leaves, ribs removed

2½ tablespoons chopped walnuts

1 garlic clove, peeled

Salt and ground black pepper

2 tablespoons extra-virgin olive oil

2 tablespoons butter, melted

2 tablespoons grated Parmesan cheese

Fill a large pot halfway with water and bring to a boil over high heat. Place the turnip greens two at a time in the boiling water for 30 seconds. Remove the leaves and drain on paper towels and pat dry. Stack the leaves on top of one another. Roll into a cigar and cut crosswise into 1-inch-wide strips.

Preheat the oven to 350°F. Place the walnuts on a baking sheet and bake until lightly toasted, about 5 minutes.

Place the turnip green strips in a food processor. Add the toasted walnuts, garlic, ½ teaspoon salt, and ⅛ teaspoon pepper. Process until it begins to form a paste, about 2 minutes. With the processor running, drizzle in oil and butter. Add the Parmesan and pulse 2 or 3 times. Season to taste with more salt and pepper. Transfer the pesto to a small bowl.

Makes about 1 cup

# Acknowledgments

WRITING A COOKBOOK HAS ALWAYS BEEN A DREAM OF MINE, and I would like to thank the three people who made it all possible for me. Thank you, Gordon Ramsay, Joe Bastianich, and Graham Elliot, for believing in me enough to name me America's first *MasterChef,* and as a result, giving me this opportunity to write my first cookbook. I owe you all my first signed copies. Thank you, Gordon, for writing the foreword for my cookbook; it has been an honor having you taste my dishes and bestow such high compliments. Adeline Ramage Rooney, thank you for all your help and advice through the challenging process of writing my first cookbook. Thank you, Chad and Kelia from Reveille, for aiding me in meeting deadlines; all the late-night e-mails were appreciated.

I have had the pleasure of working with Julie Will, my editor, who has helped me edit, organize, and assemble my recipes for the cookbook. Thanks, Julie, for all your creative inspiration and the way you stayed true to my Southern style. I am also thankful to Brys Stephens, my food tester, for testing all my recipes. From having personally cooked and measured each dish, I know that this was a big endeavor.

I had an amazing experience at my photo shoot in New York. I had a wonderful time working with Ellen Silverman. She made me feel at ease, which allowed me to appear very natural in front of the camera. Many thanks, Kevin Norris and Kara Plikaitis for helping a girl look "skinny" in her photos, making sure my clothes were smoothed and shaped to fit. Alejandra Nerizagal, I know you had a fun time taming my long locks throughout the whole day at the photo shoot. Thank you for working your makeup magic in making my eyes "pop."

Cyd McDowell, you did a great job preparing and styling the food for the pictures; you really made my recipes come to life. Thank you for your hospitality on set; my mom and I loved the sweet tea. For setting the stage for my food to look its best, I want to thank Natasha Louise King; I loved the Southern chic décor.

Thank you, Kara, Marie Crousillat, Kate Slate, Nancy N. Bailey, and Wendy Gable at Rodale, for all your assistance in putting together this cookbook. You have all been a part of making my dream come true.

Last but not least, I would like to thank all of my hometown taste testers, Mrs. Cynthia, Mrs. Glenda, Mrs. Debra, Mrs. Lori, and all of my friends, family, and acquaintances who tasted my food and inspired me to pursue my dream.

# Index

Boldfaced page references indicate photographs.

# MasterChef

*MasterChef* is the worldwide hit talent competition that sets out on a quest to find the best amateur cook in the country. Contestants on *MasterChef* are put through the paces with various challenges as they compete head-to-head to create delicious dishes. These everyday at-home cooks have the once-in-a-lifetime opportunity to show their passion and excitement for food as they are put to the test and judged by world-renowned chefs.

The series serves as a unique platform for people from all walks of life who want to follow their dream of working as a professional chef. The winner will be the chef whose passion, creativity, technical skills, and love of food means they are truly a MasterChef.